SPEAK UP
WITH
CONFIDENCE

SPEAK UP
WITH
CONFIDENCE

How to Prepare, Learn,
and Deliver
Effective Speeches

JACK VALENTI

WILLIAM MORROW AND COMPANY, INC.

New York 1982

Library of Congress Cataloging in Publication Data

Valenti, Jack.
  Speak up with confidence.

  1. Public speaking. I. Title.
PN4121.V28   808.5′1   81–22505
ISBN 0–688–01174–8   AACR2

Printed in the United States of America

First Edition

  3 4 5 6 7 8 9 10

BOOK DESIGN BY MICHAEL MAUCERI

To my family,
Mary Margaret, Courtenay, John, and Alexandra
and
to my loving friends, Anne and Kirk Douglas

CONTENTS

AN INTRODUCTORY NOTE

Anyone who wants to achieve can learn to rise before a group of people and speak with pride, conviction, and persuasion.

If you are a man or woman in business or in college; if you are interested in your community and from time to time choose to rise and speak about your concerns; if you are a public official or want to be one; if you are called to testify before city councils, state legislatures, the Congress; if you participate in the affairs of a club or civic organization—this book is aimed at you.

You can learn to speak better than you think possible.

I am not suggesting that reading this book will make you one of the nation's great platform or television speakers. But I am most assuredly saying that if you learn some simple rules, and apply those rules with personal discipline, you can achieve a level of professionalism in your speechmaking.

When you want to lose weight or master a language or become a competent skier, you don't expect any overnight miracles. You know you have to work toward your goal. By the same token, you cannot take a pill at bedtime and wake up the next day a brilliant orator.

The secret of speaking well is discipline—work, preparation. If you are unwilling to devote effort to the task, you cannot reach your goal.

You can do whatever you wish to do if you are capable of sustained concentration and take the time necessary to practice what you are learning. Obviously, these same qualities are prerequisite to playing the piano, or managing people, or reading a balance sheet, or raising a family of children in whom you can take justifiable pride.

- *Learning is work.*

- *Work is the gateway to achievement.*

- *Achievement may prompt one of the most exciting emotions you will ever feel.*

If this formula is not uncongenial to you, if you truly believe that hurdles are made to surmount, then read on.

—JACK VALENTI
Washington, D.C.

SPEAK UP
WITH
CONFIDENCE

I

THE BEGINNING

Why you must know what you are going to say

He approached the rostrum looking no less than what he was, the commanding officer of one of the largest corporations in America. Tall, tending a touch toward portliness, firm of jaw, and thick of hair, he dominated the others on the dais.

The audience, some thousand men and women in the Waldorf Astoria ballroom, waited expectantly for the words of a man they had been persuaded would offer them wisdom beyond their means about the future of the national economic landscape.

And then the blight began.

The corporate chief executive's thick, usually confident fingers clutched the sides of the speaker's lectern so as not to betray their trembling. He cleared his throat, and then, as a drowning man grabs a floating log, he leaped into the text before him, eyes fastened on the typescript, straining to keep jangling nerve ends from screeching loud enough to be heard by all in the room.

The speech was a dud.

He droned when he should have talked. The confident, imperious manner that served him so well in board rooms and staff meetings had fled. The speech he should have read over and over again to know it cold had lain unregarded in his briefcase for too long.

In short, this fine figure of a powerful business executive failed the test that ought to be applied to the leader of any enterprise: Can he stand before a group of people and persuade them, inspire them, and finally convince them?

It is a fact of life that too many people who ought to have developed some facility in speaking have done no such thing. How many public officials have you heard who seem to have brought dullness and droning to a high art?

If those who should speak well as part of their professional equipment can't do it, what about the vast majority of us who speak only occasionally? How can we be expected to do even passably well?

There is nothing really special about speaking in public. It is not a gift genetically inherited nor is it divinely inspired. The truth is that speaking well before groups is a learnable craft, just as woodworking, skiing, playing the saxophone, ballroom dancing, gardening, sex, or roller-skating is learned.

Stage fright is nothing to be ashamed of. Even the most seasoned professionals are affected by it. Actors and actresses, who make their living by performing for others, are not immune to the clammy embrace of fear. Some great actors claim that fear is a stimulant, alerting the mind and the tongue, rousing the nerve centers to a fine sensitivity, tuned to the moment's duty. Total relaxation—fearlessness, if you will—can often be delusive, slackening the responses, loosening the very fibers that ought to be taut and ready. Stage fright, then, is a spur to achievement. It is a good sign, not a bad one.

I remember well an occasion when I appeared on an Academy Award television spectacular, to present the Best Foreign

Picture award. My co-presenter was the dazzlingly beautiful actress Jacqueline Bisset. Before we were to go on, she and I were stationed backstage waiting for our cue. We chatted aimlessly. At least she did. I was so intrigued by her, by her poise, her serene loveliness, and the graceful way she stood quietly, that I may have exposed my own nervousness, caused less by anticipation of our appearance on stage than by the fact that I was meeting and talking with her for the first time. As one does in moments like these, I resorted to small talk.

"It's interesting," I began, "that you will soon be visible to more people tonight than have seen all your movies, everywhere. There'll be about four hundred million people watching us tonight, here and around the world."

Her marvelously sculptured face suddenly grew taut. "My God," she exclaimed, "you shouldn't say things like that now. Four hundred million people!" The thought of that vast unseen populace struck her with noticeable impact. While the audience in the theater numbered some three thousand (a manageable group, I suspect, to an experienced actress) the possibility of fouling up lines before that terrifyingly large and surely attentive mass of viewers out there was a matter of more than casual concern. This was a "live" show—no second or third takes, but live—and that meant the first time was the only time.

Soon we were summoned to the edge of the back curtain by one of the assistant directors. "You'll go on next," he whispered. I nodded. Miss Bisset's smile was thin. Then we were being introduced, and we walked toward the Plexiglas rostrum, from which protruded two long, slim microphones. The lights were intense, blotting out for a brief moment the seated audience, among whom were fabled personalities in motion pictures and television.

As we stood in our appointed places, I was to begin the dialogue. A bare second before I spoke, for some unaccountable reason I noticed her left hand resting on the lectern. It was trembling. Immediately I had the horrible thought that if this professional actress, so accustomed to performing before others, was in a state of—how shall I say—semi-fright, why on earth wasn't I? And, on the instant, I was.

But a heart-quiver later, the mysterious mechanism that pumps whatever it is that lubricates the mind, preparing words to slide effortlessly from their hiding places and burst forth in coherent speech, cranked up and I was speaking. It is also cheering to report that Miss Bisset never missed a beat. The professionalism that sustained her was in good working order and we finished our presentation, without fault and on time.

When we were done, I suddenly felt that inexpressible relief that comes to athletes, soldiers, performers, who have accomplished their assigned task in the face of threatened disaster. It was over and it had gone well. Miss Bisset, having overcome her momentary concern, was never more lovely.

I wondered about that for some time.

I considered my own state of mind. Watching her trembling hand could have thrown me off; it almost did. Why didn't it? The reason, I reflected, was quite simple: I was thoroughly prepared. I was confident that I knew what I was going to say, even though there was always the crutch of cue cards.

(It is no revelation to observant viewers of the Academy Award ceremonies that there are immense cards beneath the lens of the camera positioned in the center of the auditorium. On these cards each presenter's dialogue is printed in a size that even the most myopic would find it hard to miss. The Academy Award producers, having small faith in the chancy nature of memory, provide a mnemonic safety net. Under the circumstances, the only way to flub one's dialogue is to be unable to read English. That such mishaps have occurred on Academy Award shows only certifies that if something can go wrong, it usually does. Particularly if one is negligent about preparation.)

The most effective antidote to stage fright and other calamities of speechmaking is total, slavish, monkish preparation.

I had memorized my thirty-second part. (Pitifully small, but then again, when four hundred million people out there are waiting for you to fall on your backside—even one as shapely as Miss Bisset's—thirty seconds can be an eternity.)

I had gone over the lines again, and again, and again, and again. I lost count of how many times I said those lines. I said them in the shower, as I was drying, as I was shaving, as I was sitting on an airplane. I could have said them backward (God, the horror of actually doing that). But the central fact was that I knew them, knew them cold, and the knowledge was like a warm embrace. It comforted me. It sustained me through any untoward incident, even the trembling hand of a beautiful professional actress.

The first, the foremost, the indispensable step in making a speech—any kind of speech, whether it is a two-line introduction of another speaker, or a toast after dinner, or a formal presentation to a large convention, or a report to the Kiwanis Club on the state of the treasury, or the proposal of a budget for a board of directors—is to *know what you are going to say.*

I have been on a number of Academy Award television shows and have been astonished on several occasions to see film pros stumble, even with cue cards, and sometimes wander off into improvisations that curdled the blood of the director.

Why?

The explanation is simple: lack of preparation, casual neglect of essentials, failing to become thoroughly acquainted with what you are supposed to say.

If dedicated professionals can fall prey to this omission, then nonprofessionals must take special care. Getting ready for the speech is the first requirement. Without it, only the oratorically talented can survive. With it, every person who chooses to can be a satisfactory speaker.

It goes without saying that any counsel contained in this volume is directed equally to men and to women. Though there is some statistical evidence that women tend to have greater difficulty with public speaking than men do. Colette Dowling, in her insightful book *The Cinderella Complex*, writes:

Many women also feel intense anxiety over public speaking. In a survey of 200 students training to become psychoanalysts at the William Alanson White Institute, Ruth Moulton, a senior training analyst there (she is also on the faculty of Columbia University), found that 50% of the women tested were unable to speak in public as compared with 20% of the men. For some women, the anxiety was so overwhelming it produced attacks of dizziness and fainting. In trying to state their positions, some women become confused, forget what they wanted to say, can't find the right word, won't look people in the eye. Or they blush, stutter, or find that their voices quaver the minute someone disagrees with them.

Preparation, exacting and minute, might prove an antidote to the fear these women experience. Without it, Ms. Dowling's catalogue of tremors can be suffered equally by men.

Remember: You do not have to be a professional to make a good speech, but you do have to prepare. Very seldom will you be called on to speak without warning. If you have an assigned part on a program, you know it in advance. You should also know the nature of your audience and your subject. Thus armed, anyone can learn to speak passably well and, more importantly, can continue to perfect his or her skills on an ever-ascending curve.

II

THE PREPARATION

How to be ready to say what you want to say

There are three methods of speaking.

One, without notes. (This is for the old pros, not for beginners. It is like trying to schuss down a steep ski slope the first time you put on skis. You will spend more time on your backside than you will skiing.)

Second, with notes that give you an outline of what you have prepared to say, but no details.

Third, from a prepared text.

Let us begin with a prepared text. Later on we will pursue in some detail how to write a speech, but first we will concentrate on the preparation.

The first step is to have your speech typed *in exactly the form you will use.*

Do *not* practice a speech that has been put down on paper in a form (that is, paragraphing and spacing) that is different from the reading copy you will use.

Break up the speech into paragraphs—short paragraphs. You will also find it useful to skip an extra line between paragraphs so that each may be seen as a separate, self-contained entity.

The speech should be composed so that each paragraph is concerned with one thought. The first sentence in the paragraph should serve as a signal for what follows. It is the banner behind which the rest of the paragraph will march in serried and connected ranks.

Read over your speech. Read it once, twice, three times. Read it fifty times! Read it so often that it is almost committed to memory, though you need not go that far.

The trick is to read your speech so many times that the words are like old friends. You know them so well that each word is familiar to you, not some alien shape that takes you by surprise. And each word you speak will immediately nudge you into recognizing the next word. Suddenly these old companions will be on your lips, formed easily and without fear.

If you have trouble pronouncing a specific word, take it out and insert another word that is more comfortable for you. There are some 400,000 words in the English language. Don't be afraid to edit, so that every word in the speech is one with which you feel at ease. Stumbling over a word or two sounds an alarm bell that alerts your audience to impending disaster. A mispronounced word, a word too ungainly for you to handle correctly, puts whatever follows in jeopardy. Avoid words with hissing sounds, or vowel and consonant juxtapositions that cause your tongue to become slovenly.

When I was in charge of President Lyndon Johnson's speech-writing staff, I pursued such words with the vigilance of a beagle on point. Whenever I wrote a speech for the President, I was overly cautious about using any word or name that had oral "thorns" on it. In editing and revising staff-written speeches, I went to extraordinary lengths to sniff out and excise such verbal briers. The President grew surly when we were going over a speech and he came across a word that some overliterate speech draftsman had constructed. He would invariably say, "What in the hell are you trying to do to me? Get that goddamn word out of there." The President, like so many of us, had difficulty with cumbersome words, and words with foreign derivations. I remember "nuance," which he persistently brought forth as "new ants." Terror is the only term adequate to describe my feelings when I recall that I once failed to edit that word out of a presidential speech. That neglect later elicited one of the President's more awesome reactions in his appraisal of the author. I forget his exact words only because my conscience is easily outraged.

Now, read your speech over and over and over again. Read it until the words have become so settled in your mind you have no hesitancy in approaching each of them with easy familiarity.

After you have read the speech sufficiently to acquire this facility, next read the speech by paragraphs. Read the first paragraph again and again.

Then to the second paragraph. Again, the key words should carry you easily through the rest of the paragraph.

The same attention goes into the rest of the speech.

Why? Why this drudging repetition?

Because you will soon make a strange, emancipating discovery. The mind is like a camera. It can photograph chunks of prose. If you have persistently aimed the camera of your eyes at each paragraph, the eye and the brain make an imprint of what you are reading. If you do this often enough, you can lift your gaze from the copy and almost see, in the retina of the eye, a positive reflection of what is on the paper. It is this "photographing" of each paragraph that will give you a special asset that separates good speakers from merely adequate or bad speakers. You will be able to lift your eyes from your text to make contact with your audience.

That is why the text you rehearse should be spaced and paragraphed exactly as you will deliver it. The mind will have "photographed" these paragraph chunks ahead of time; if you disarrange the paragraphing, you will blur the photograph.

Don't hesitate to use capitalization and <u>underlines</u> in your written text to let you know when to emphasize, as well as to help you lift that sentence or word out of the speech for "special handling."

Underlining, capital letters, dashes, even circling a word or two, help you keep the rhythm alive. They are crutches to keep you from stumbling.

These are the speech aids of professionals. They make the difference between a mediocre speech, laggardly delivered, and a good speech, balanced, keyed, cadenced, to lend to the substance of your written text the dynamism of the spoken word.

Let me take you through a speech that may be rightly valued as one of the finest examples of American oratory in this century, the inaugural address of John F. Kennedy, at the East Front of the Capitol, January 20, 1961.

I have abridged the speech and inserted in the lines the kinds of aids you can use. Practice this speech yourself, to see how you would deliver it.

We observe today <u>not</u> a victory of party, but a celebration of freedom — symbolizing an <u>end</u> as well as a <u>beginning</u> — signifying <u>renewal</u> — as well as <u>change</u>.

For I have sworn before you <u>and</u> Almighty God the <u>same</u> solemn oath our forebears prescribed nearly a century and three quarters ago.

The world is <u>very</u> different now.

For man holds in his mortal hands the power to abolish <u>all</u> forms of human poverty — <u>AND</u> all forms of human life.

And yet, the same revolutionary beliefs for which our forebears fought are still at issue around the globe — the belief that the <u>rights of man</u> come <u>NOT</u> from the generosity of the state — but from the <u>hand</u> of God.

Note that I have reparagraphed the sentences. Underlines mark those words that need to be punctuated with your voice. The dashes represent those oh-so-brief pauses that give a little more lilt and emphasis to the clauses or sentences that follow. The pauses are almost imperceptible, but they are there to give special force to what is being said.

If you have "photographed" the speech in your mind, when your eyes fasten on the first phrase—"We observe today <u>not</u> a victory of party"—you will be able to raise your eyes to look at the audience (and the camera) as you say "symbolizing an <u>end</u> as well as a <u>beginning</u>"; the eyes drop ever so briefly to pick up the next phrase—"signifying <u>renewal</u>"—and then are raised again as you speak the last clause, "as well as <u>change</u>."

Carry on with the next paragraph, an easy one to handle without reading more than the first few words.

Continue through the speech, the very brief glance down to pick up the key words in the next sentence, then looking up again to speak the rest of the words.

Go on to Kennedy's next paragraph.

We dare not forget today that we are the heirs of that <u>first</u> revolution.

Let the word go forth <u>from this time</u> — and <u>from this place</u> — to friends and foes alike — that the torch has passed to a NEW generation of Americans — <u>born</u> in this century — <u>tempered</u> by war — <u>disciplined</u> by a hard and bitter peace — <u>proud</u> of our ancient heritage — and <u>unwilling</u> to witness or permit the slow undoing of those human rights to which this nation has <u>always</u> been committed — and to which we are committed <u>today</u> — at <u>home</u> and around the <u>world</u>.

The key phrases are lifted out—emphasized—and held up for the audience to hear and understand.

The first sentence is the standard-bearer of what is to follow. Thus, when the phrase "let the word go forth <u>from this time</u> and <u>from this place</u>" is spoken, it is opening the door to what is to follow, the eloquence of the short, vivid phrases.

When the words are strung together, the mounting drama of the speech is softened, permitted to go a touch lax, but if they are framed by an ever-so-brief pause, there is heft to the words.

Continue now to the paragraph oft quoted in the years that followed, sometimes in criticism of the President's theme (by those who quarreled at a later time about Vietnam and America's role as world policeman) but never to discredit the splendor of the words.

Let <u>every</u> nation know — whether it wishes us <u>well</u> or <u>ill</u> — that we will pay <u>any</u> price — bear <u>any</u> burden — meet <u>any</u> hardship — support <u>any</u> friend — oppose <u>any</u> foe — to assure the <u>survival</u> and the <u>success</u> of liberty.

There is imposed here a deliberate rhythm that is the mark of a truly great speech. The rise and fall of the clauses, the immediacy of the moment, the heightening of intensity.

Rhythm, like the fluid movements of a great dancer or superb athlete, is essential to the graceful exposition of a line, a thought, or a theme.

Sentences must not collide with one another, thereby breaking up their rhythm. Edward Bennett Williams, the celebrated

Washington attorney, once mused about how he had learned the prime importance of not bunching his prose in one congealed hunk. "Mrs. Fitzgerald, my English teacher in high school," he recalled, "would rap my knuckles when I indulged in SRT (sentences running together). I used to flunk law students when I taught law at Yale and Georgetown when they could not express themselves correctly. Of course"—he grinned—"you can't flunk students today on that count."

In a monograph on music, Alan Rich wrote: "The composer satisfied memory by furnishing the listener with memorable materials (usually a melody but just as easily a sonority, a rhythm, or even, conceivably, a certain length of silence) and by bringing back those materials from time to time to let the listeners become oriented and suspect the presence of an orderly process of departure and return. Sometimes the materials are returned verbatim, sometimes they are altered."

This is the measure of the importance of rhythm in speaking.

Now, to the denouement of the JFK speech, and its most rememberable line:

> And so my fellow Americans — ask not what your country can do for you — ask what you can do for your country.

And so on to the closing lines:

> With a good conscience our only sure reward — with history the final judge of our deeds — let us go forth to lead the land we love — asking His blessing and His help — but knowing that here on earth God's work must be truly our own.

The eye picks up the first phrase—"With a good conscience our only sure reward." Now lift your eyes to challenge your audience with a full gaze as you speak the next line. Your need to return to the typescript will depend on how thorough your preparation has been. Remember that the rhythm of your speaking voice will be affected by the direction of your gaze. *Never* read. Use your eyes—and your thorough preparation—to let the text be a guide, not your sole means of support.

Anyone who chooses to be professional in the delivery of a speech should take one more preparatory step. Speak what you intend to say into a tape recorder, in front of a mirror, so that you can practice both eye contact with the audience and the rhythm and cadence of your vocal presentation. Time yourself with a stopwatch, if you can, to keep track of the length of your speech.

This practice is the best preparatory work you can do.

First: Read over the text several times; read it out loud. Try to get the feel of the words, and connect the ideas so that you feel comfortable with what you are saying.

Second: Stand in front of a mirror. Either hold the text in your hands at about the level of a lectern or place it on a table high enough to resemble a lectern.

Third: Begin to read your speech. This time, however, start the rhythm of looking down at the first line, speaking it, and then letting your eye pick up the next several words or the next complete sentence. Now bring your eyes up to face your image in the mirror as you speak the next few words or sentence. Eyes back to the text as you speak the next line; then repeat the sequence: Let your eyes "float" ahead to pick up the next sentence, and look up to face your audience.

Fourth: Continue this pattern through the entire speech.

Don't worry about stumbling or forgetting. This is practice, and in practice you are aiming to get the feel and the sense of your speech. The time to make errors or to be awkward is in these practice moments.

Fifth: Consider what you have done. Do you think you have managed to confront your audience at least half the time? That is, have you made eye contact as often and for as long as you have been buried in your text?
Think about this and be honest with yourself. Then begin again and repeat the sequence.

Sixth: Try in the next practice sessions to increase the time of eye contact with the audience and lessen the time of reading. Do it again and again.
You will discover that you can, after a while, increase substantially the percentage of time in which your eyes are on your audience and not on your text. There is no cause for you to feel as if you are walking a tightrope across the Grand Canyon—your text is there before you, a nice soft mattress for you to fall on. But eventually, as your percentage improves, your own sense of confidence (and exhilaration) will ascend dramatically.

Seventh: Once you feel comfortable with the speech, concentrate on the sound of your voice and the emphasis you give to those phrases you want to point up for your audience in order to persuade them.

Eighth: Consider the overall time of your speech. You may want to edit your text to decrease the total speaking time.

I can pledge you that all this drudgery—and sometimes it may seem precisely that—has a splendid payoff. When you stand before whatever group you address, you will be more confident, more poised than you thought possible, and when you are done, you will probably give your performance a higher rating than you had previously imagined you could. There are few experiences you will savor with more exquisite aftertaste than the successful delivery of a good speech to a responsive audience. Particularly satisfying is the knowledge that because you prepared yourself with rigorous attention to detail, unaided by partners or group effort or grant of favor from any benefactor, you mastered the moment and were, for a brief span of time, triumphant.

It is absolutely essential that you look at your audience. You must not bury your face in your printed text, ignoring the living, breathing people in front of you. Even when you have to drop your gaze to pick up a word or two, suspend contact with the audience for only a few moments.

To do this with ease, you must prepare, practice. There is no known substitute for preparation.

How often—oh, God, how often?—have you sat and listened to a speaker trudge monotonously on, eyes fastened to reading text, voice focused on typescript, clutching each word, and losing all rapport with an audience that by now have stopped looking at their watches and have started to examine the calendar.

My old friend David Brinkley, among the two or three best network news anchor men ever to preside over an evening news show, once amusedly described to me his appearance at a meeting of the Illinois Bankers Association. Brinkley's turn at the rostrum was preceded by a fellow lugging a large briefcase, which he proceeded to place on top of the lectern; he opened it, thrashed through it, pages fluttering, knocked over a water glass, and finally extracted from beneath the pile the speech he was looking for. It was a ten-page document, and the gentleman, provided with neither humor nor eye contact, proceeded to read the entire speech, causing terminal fatigue to run through the audience like a viral contagion. Brinkley sat in horror, mixed with genuine awe that anyone could so continue without apparent frustration or embarrassment.

In preparing a speech from a written text, you cannot spend too much time burning every word into your memory. Photograph every paragraph in your mind.

The eight-step preparatory exercise outlined on pages 25–26 can be your escape from the written text. When you are no longer a slave to print, the audience will rejoice in your freedom. If you have prepared sufficiently, I warrant you that it is quite possible to drop your eyes seldom and then only to refresh your vision of your "photograph."

Too many high-stationed business executives forage among balance sheets and variable budgets with unerring instinct, but inflict on audiences what *New York Times* columnist Bill Safire has described as MEGO (My Eyes Glaze Over). The quality of public speaking in the American business community is on a level lower than can be measured by most precision instruments. I have been witness to performances of chairmen and presidents—men who stride their corporate corridors with firm and decisive step but, when on a speaker's rostrum, combine all the lesser traits of Mush Mouth Mulligan with the inspiration of a fellow reciting the latest Lithuanian bond prices.

Alongside corporate captains, place great scientists, labor leaders, and Nobel Prize winners. This country is long on elected officials who address eager audiences ready to be informed and inspired—and soon those present are measuring the distance to the nearest exit. I recall listening to an influential labor leader who commanded the legions of one of the most important unions in the nation. I now understand why his colleagues used to say, "He can empty a hall faster than someone shouting *fire!*"

Making contact with an audience with your eyes is not a guarantee of inspired oratory. But you will have eliminated the largest deterrent to a satisfactory speech. You will have held at least a portion of their interest, because you have not cut the lifeline to their attention.

Louis Nizer, the famous courtroom attorney and one of the finest platform speakers in America (whose book *Thinking on Your Feet* is a classic in the art of speaking) wrote in his autobiography, *Reflections Without Mirrors:*

> Professor John Dewey drew large classes at Columbia College because of his eminence, but he suffered the highest absences. He was as dull orally as he was profound in his writings. Professor Albert Einstein did not need the aid of his accent to be incomprehensible. His eyes were buried in his script. His words in monotone emerged haltingly from behind his mustache, losing volume as they were sifted through hair. Audiences rushed to see and hear him, and after they had satisfied their eyes, they closed their ears. Ultimately, they turned to small talk among themselves while the great man droned on. His best oration was at a commencement exercise where he was one of the speakers. He arose and said, "I do not have any particular thoughts to express today, so I wish you all success in your future years." Then he sat down. If only others who had nothing to say would follow his example.

The speaker must see his audience, look into their eyes, observe their facial expressions, and communicate directly to them as participants.

Those of us who remember President John F. Kennedy delivering his inaugural address can readily recall the excitement that brought fire to our veins as the young President spoke. His face, alive and passionate, was lifted toward his audience, drawing us to him, extinguishing our fears, revitalizing our faith. He talked to us, not to his text.

Yet I also remember the first time I heard John Kennedy speak, sometime in 1956. He focused on his text, voiced in an unfamiliar accent (in Texas we found his pronounciation odd), plunging ahead with head bowed over the typescript of his speech; our center of attention was the top of his full head of thickly gardened brown hair, since that was the portion of him most visible to his auditors.

James MacGregor Burns, historian and chronicler of the Kennedy years, once wrote of Senator John Kennedy's maiden speech in the Senate on May 18, 1953:

> Loaded with facts and specific proposals (for New England) the speech sounded very much like an economics lecture at the Harvard Business School. Kennedy spurned rhetoric and oratorical eloquence. He did not bother with any stories, jokes or even illustrative references for "human interest." He simply drove straight along his course.

But Kennedy determined that he would do better. Early on he recognized that he needed another arrow in his quiver: He would apply his talents to becoming a good speaker. His own natural skills were brought to a high polish. He quickly realized that when all else failed, a ready humor would cover mistakes and defuse a hostile audience.

When campaigning for the presidency, he began to develop and practice his art.

At a press conference, a reporter dropped a grenade on him. "Do you think a Protestant can be elected President in 1960?" As the transcript recorded, "Laughter."

Kennedy smiled warmly and said: "If he's prepared to answer how he stands on the issue of the separation of the Church and State, I see no reason why we should discriminate against him."

The entire press corps broke up in a howl of laughter.

In the span of time between 1956 and his inaugural in 1960, he perfected a style of speaking that was replete with wit and urbanity, and most of all, he acquired the ability to find his way through a prepared text without clinging to it, as a frightened child clutches his mother's skirt.

He learned. So can you.

While style and rhythm are important, the gritty details of the speaking environment matter too. Professional speakers and public officials all know this.

Requisite to any well-delivered speech, beyond the essentials of preparation, is to know where you are speaking, to whom you are speaking, the logistics and layout of the hall, and the atmosphere of the event.

Keep a checklist of items you want to know about *in advance.*

1. Where is the speech to be delivered? Is it in a large room or a small one? How many people will be in attendance? If it is a small room, can you dispense with a microphone and still be audible to the assembled people? If a microphone is indicat-

ed, do you want a stand-up, a lavaliere (to be hung around your neck), or a hand-held mike with a long cord?

2. Always ask for a lectern of some kind, unless you are going to speak without notes. The lectern is useful in two ways: It can hold your notes or text, and it is a pillar, a life-preserver if you don't know what to do with your hands. You can hold on to its sides. You can lean against it. Whatever you feel most comfortable with, whatever eases your nervousness and makes you feel better about speaking, make use of.

3. What kind of audience is this? Are they a homogenous group—that is, do they all come to hear you because of a shared interest—or are they from differing groups and backgrounds? For example, you may be speaking to the local Lion's Club. They are members of the same club but they all come from disparate backgrounds. On the other hand, if you are speaking to the local chapter of the Cost Accountants Association, your audience has at least one connecting link that binds them together. You need to know who the audience is, and why they have assembled.

Whatever the topic of your speech, always try to insert in the beginning of the speech (or in the middle, where it is least expected) some inside joke or thought particularly pertinent to the people who listen to you. Whether they are bankers or security analysts or meat-packers, find out something about them, their business, some of their best-known leaders, and add to your text a few lines directly targeted to this particular audience. You are guaranteed an appreciative, embracing response.

4. What is the format? Who will introduce you? Are you the only speaker? If not, who precedes you and who follows you, and what are they speaking about? If the format is a panel discussion, who are your fellow panel members, and how is the panel to operate?

5. What is your subject to be and how much time is allocated to your part of the program? Always try to give back a few minutes of the allotted time. Nothing so surprises—and gratifies—arranging committees as to deal with a speaker who is eager to shorten rather than lengthen time allotments.

6. Are you speaking from a platform or is there some other arrangement? Will the audience be seated entirely in front of you or will they surround you, as in a theater in the round? Is there to be a head table, or will you rise and speak at your own table, or are you to sit in the audience until you are called to speak? Do you wait until you have been formally introduced to go to the rostrum, or do you sit in a designated location near the introducer?

7. Will there be a question-and-answer period, and if so, how long will it be? How are the mechanics of recognizing the questioners to be handled? Will they rise in the audience, or are their questions to be written out in advance and handed up to the chairman to read aloud? Who will call a halt to the questions, and in what manner? (You should never end the question period yourself, but always arrange in advance for the chairman to shut off the audience response.)

8. Are you speaking at a luncheon or dinner, or at a business meeting of some kind? If no formal meal is involved, will refreshments be served before, or during, the meeting? At what time will you go on?

If you are an after-dinner speaker keep in mind several points:

People who have been sitting for over an hour, pouring down drinks, eating heartily, talking incessantly to their dinner companions, are not usually eager to be regaled with a long program. After-dinner speaking is the toughest obstacle course to traverse successfully. This is the time for a brief speech, never longer than fifteen minutes. The shorter the speech, the more merciful you will appear to your audience and the more enthusiastically they will applaud your understanding of their plight. They are hostages praying for release.

For an after-dinner speech, always find out the order of the program. If you have a choice, be the first to speak after the meal. Dinner guests will be more attentive and a bit more appreciative of the first speaker. Their enthusiasm and their patience decrease with each speaker who follows.

If you are to be an after-luncheon speaker, always remember that 2:00 P.M. is the favorite quitting time. If you can't finish by 2:00 P.M., finish anyway, or you will be bedeviled by the shuffling of chairs and the hunched-over exit of a good many in your audience. While you may know that what you are saying is well worth listening to, the clock is inexorable and deaf to your voice.

9. Finally, be prepared in advance to respond to a lavish introduction. First, you should keep your eyes on the person introducing you, so that if the introduction is particularly flowery, you can avoid embarrassment by avoiding the eyes of the audience. Second, you should smile deprecatingly when the introducer carries on a little too fulsomely about your achievements and your splendid charm. Let the audience know that you know the speaker is laying it on a bit thick.

Another advantage accrues from keeping your gaze on the person introducing you. Your own first eye contact with the audience becomes a little more dramatic when you rise to speak—you are now "seeing" them for the first time, and you are in command of their full attention.

In summary, attention to every detail is the mark of a professional, of someone who cares very much about doing the best job possible. Only by knowing all there is to know about your subject, your audience, the environment of the meeting, the type and timing of the program, and your own well-thought-out plan of response, will you be sufficiently armed to take up the challenge and be successful. You will never fall through a crack in the floor if you have mapped the territory in advance.

III

THE LENGTH

How long you should speak, and why you should not speak long

The best way to begin this chapter is to quote a gentleman who was the first—other than the prophets of the Bible—to declare the value of a compact speech. Saint Ambrose, Bishop of Milan in the fourth century, wrote, "Let us have a reason for beginning and let our end be within due limits. For a speech that is wearisome only stirs up anger."

To the reasons for Saint Ambrose's canonization please add his full appreciation of the value of brevity and substance.

It is my conviction, based on years of being put upon by all manner of public speakers, that *twenty minutes is the absolute maximum* that anyone should allow for a speech. It is a known fact that Fidel Castro and Leonid Brezhnev inflict on their audiences speeches of an hour, even two or three hours. Indeed, it is recorded that on his ascendancy to the post of Chairman of the Communist Party in the People's Republic of China (formerly occupied by Mao Zedong), Hua Guofeng spoke to the

41

faithful for over three and a half hours. It is also a known fact that those who listen to such leaders have meager alternatives.

The late Hubert Humphrey, perhaps the greatest public speaker this country has known in this century, was notorious for going beyond what may be judged the absolute limit. I have listened innumerable times to Senator Humphrey. When I was part of his campaign entourage in 1968, on more than one occasion I counted as many as eight "climax" opportunities, when if he had bowed and said thank you, he would have concluded in a blaze of glory. But each time, the irrepressible senator (then Vice President) continued on, sweeping to a new curve of oratory while the audience, ready to applaud, sat back again and waited. And waited.

But Humphrey was an anomaly, an original. He seldom spoke from a written text, preferring to extemporize, an ability born of countless hours on the stump, where he honed and perfected his special style. Humphrey was one of the few speakers I know who could invest his speech with humor, self-deprecating, belly-splitting humor, without the aid of professional funnymen. Like most originals he broke every rule in the book, and got away with it, because he possessed inexhaustible resources of eloquence, and made skillful and awe-inspiring use of what Francis Bacon once described as "the choiceness of the phrase, the round and clean composition of the sentence, and the sweet falling of the clauses."

Before mounting the speaker's rostrum, make sure you have practiced your written speech not only for form, memory, and familiarity, but also for time. A rule of thumb is that one 8½ by 11 typed page, double-spaced, will hold about two minutes' worth of spoken material. Therefore, you can usually judge that eight pages of script will run about sixteen minutes. But practice and practice again. If you find your speech rhythms run more than two minutes per page, edit, cut, reduce. Keep the speech under twenty minutes—fifteen is more desirable, and ten minutes is great. Remember this maxim: *It is very difficult to make a bad speech out of a short speech.*

Even the most talented speakers fall prey to the "endless" speech. I recall I was once invited to sit on the dais at a mammoth gathering sponsored by the prestigious City Club of New York and honoring that evening Charles Bluhdorn, the colorful and successful chairman of the board of Gulf & Western, a prosperous and diverse corporation. The featured speaker was Daniel Patrick Moynihan, then the U.S. Ambassador to the United Nations, now an influential senator from New York.

Pat Moynihan is a rarity, a gifted intellectual and orator brimming over with a wild Irish wit, a prodigal elfin charm that mixes with his own unique recipe of literate bite and splendor. This evening, however, Moynihan delivered a civics lecture, erudite, packed with statistics ill-suited to an audience heavily weighted with business proconsuls who had a low threshold of interest in the socioeconomics of urban sprawl—a speech altogether more fitting for an auditoriumful of Harvard doctoral candidates. He spoke for over forty minutes, and during the last twenty-five there was restlessness among the natives. When he finally finished, the sighs of relief could have inflated the Graf zeppelin. Moynihan came with a deserved reputation as a wit and a charmer and left with the—also deserved—label of "professor."

Some months later I heard Pat Moynihan on a live TV show in New York. He was absolutely brilliant. He spoke concisely, each word splendidly apt, and tossed off witty sentence endings with the grace of a verbal Baryshnikov. It was his brevity that gave force to what he said.

How to explain the City Club speech? Even Ted Williams and Joe DiMaggio used to strike out occasionally.

In 1980, I was one of those on a glittering dais at the annual meeting of the Friars Club (a show-business-oriented organization), honoring Henry Kissinger. In the Grand Ballroom of the Waldorf-Astoria in New York, the audience was composed of the well-known, the well-heeled, and the short-patienced. Kirk Douglas was master of ceremonies and I took the cautionary measure of consulting with him ahead of time. How many speakers, Kirk? Nine? Ye gods, then when do I go on? Number six? Ouch, that I don't like. Who is first on the program? Barbara Walters? Okay, then, let me go on second. Can you do that? That's fine.

On the dais was an array of the famous: Gregory Peck; William Buckley; the ambassadors of Egypt and Israel; the great designer Mollie Parnis; Roger Moore of James Bond fame; Frank Sinatra; Mike Wallace; movie mogul Barry Diller, chairman of Paramount Pictures; network chieftains Fred Silverman, Herb Schlosser, Brandon Tartikoff; former New York Mayor Robert Wagner; and assorted other folks well known to newspaper readers and television viewers. Also, a comedian-singer waiting in the wings to entertain.

The audience awaiting this lineup of movie stars, television commentators, and the fabled in public affairs and journalism would be eager to hear them out—until the mesmerizing enchantment wore off and ennui began to infect the hall.

Barbara Walters rose and in two and a half minutes issued a most congenial and witty presentation.

I got to my feet, tongue readied for a one-minute thirty-second essay. Barbara had set a standard for brevity that I vowed to uphold, even to surpass.

My offering:

Only in America—only in America!
Born in middle Europe, the young lad immigrates to

America and learns a second language, which even now gives off in every sentence he speaks the aroma of his origins.

The boy grown to manhood becomes a professor at one of the most prestigious universities in the United States. He writes books with persuasive designs to bring harmony to a disordered world. Washington's foreign-policy makers counsel with him, and then one day his political party, after eight years in exile, returns to power, and with the new President he comes to Washington, this time garmented in the powerful robes of National Security Adviser to the President of the United States. This foreign-born immigrant is now the chief architect of foreign policy. I salute the man who has lived this life: Zbigniew Brzezinski!

A frail piece of humor, dear Henry. For I bear you great affection and respect.

"For no man knows better how to be luminous, or how to be obscure."

This is you, Henry, and if Lord Macaulay had not written those words about William Pitt the Younger, I like to believe that I would have written them about you.

I confess to limitations, one of which is plainly the absence of any talent for stand-up comedy. Whenever I try to be humorous, it is only for a sentence or two, never more than a paragraph. Sustaining a comedic theme may seem easy. It is not.

Therefore, I got on and got off as quickly as I could. I am pleased to note I garnered one laugh, and one chuckle abandoned before it got to the belly-churning stage. For me, not a bad catch.

As I could have predicted, the example of brevity set by Barbara and me was not long emulated. Two more speakers were admirably brief, and then the clock turned into a calendar. One speaker, who shall remain nameless, to my horror plucked from his inside pocket what looked to be a sheaf of documents suitable for a legal deposition. He placed them on the rostrum and galloped off into a discourse about the fate of the land that had only sporadic relevance to the guest of honor. He was followed by two others who between them consumed twenty-five more minutes, and one could have charted on a graph the descending, soon to be avalanching, level of interest on the part of the audience, culminating in a nodding of heads and blinking of heavy lids.

But lessons of brevity are learned by bitter experience.

One year earlier, the Friars Club's annual dinner had been in honor of Johnny Carson. As it would be again, the dais was laden with the best-known people in the land. Then, too, there were eight or nine speakers, and the inevitable entertainer. The night wore on. When the entertainer finally bounded onto the stage to do his bit, I could see Johnny Carson looking at his watch. When the singular performer of this generation checks his watch, you know there is a heavy sea ahead.

When Carson at last got to his feet, smiling wanly, the crowd stirred in reawakened interest. The nonpareil Carson jauntily offered a few funny lines, then a few serious lines, thanked the Friars and the audience for their honor, and promptly sat down. The old pro had sniffed the air and resolved to flush out just one covey of laughs and call it a night.

Interminable programs are an affliction that have no known cure.

In Los Angeles, Don Rickles was the principal speaker at a meeting of a group of medical men and women. The selection of Don Rickles as the main attraction does bespeak a certain courage—not to say foolhardiness—among the medical profession, but there was a lengthy program before Mr. Rickles came on. The program came down with lingering filibusteritis. It went on and on, and many doctors in the audience with early morning appointments quietly shuffled out of the hall.

Some minutes past midnight when Rickles was called on to do his number, he rose, glared at the now diminished but hardy crowd, leaned in to the microphone, and speared the program's architect with: "Let's face it, folks. This evening just fell on its ass."

The shorter the speech, the better your chances of success. President Johnson used to instruct his staff: "Always leave at the height of a party." By this he meant, wherever you are, stop talking when your listeners expect, and want, you to keep going.

Let me summarize about length:

1. If you are speaking after dinner at a large gathering of several hundred people who have already endured a long cocktail hour and exhausted all their conversational charm on the person next to them, keep your speech *under fifteen minutes.* If you are the only speaker on the program, with perhaps some minor and brief presentations, you can extend to the twenty-minute boundary, but after that you are swimming in a riptide.

2. If you are one of several after-dinner speakers, and indeed may also share the platform with some entertainment, your remarks should be *under five minutes* in length. There are few more foolhardy acts than to drone on for ten minutes or more when you are preceded and followed by others who may follow your bad example—to your eventual dismay.

3. If you are speaking to a college class, or are the only speaker at a seminar or a forum convened for the sole purpose of hearing you, then you may and should extend your remarks to thirty minutes or more. When the chairman of such an event allots you forty-five minutes to an hour, smile politely and resolve to give him back a portion of that time. You will win

the hearts of your audience and you may devote whatever time is left to questions and answers.

4. If you are an after-luncheon speaker, there is usually a set time for adjournment. Keep your eye on your watch, and when you are introduced you will know precisely how much time is left. Even if your chairman is a lenient and hospitable fellow who says you may go beyond the quitting time, don't. I warrant you that if you continue beyond the cutoff hour you will be greeted by the thump of departing feet. *Get off on time.*

5. If you are speaking at a business, professional, or technical convention, always remember that you are only one of a legion of folks who will harangue the gathering. Keep what you are going to say compact and to the point. If you appear at a morning session after a long night of socializing by most of the convention participants, it is a certifiable fact that an interminable lecture will be as welcome as wild elephants mating in the living room. Measure the length of your talk by its nature: In a technical seminar where the audience has come to learn specifically what you have come to teach, you may extend your time with small fear of audience boredom. But if your subject is not concretely defined and detailed, be wary, and be brief. At such conventions question-and-answer periods fill in any unwelcome gaps.

IV

THE DELIVERY

How to speak with notes and without them

The ultimate ambition of a good speaker is to create rapport with the audience. What a decisive piece of language is that French word *rapport*. *Rapport* is an embrace, an affectionate warmth, a mutual reaching out, a harmonious friendliness that is the warranty of affinity and concord among people.

The prime element in constructing rapport is eye contact with those who are listening to you. Therefore, the less you refer to notes, the more you make that indispensable eye contact, the first source of rapport with your audience.

Moreover, the audience senses that a written text could have been composed by someone other than the speaker (in many cases it is). They tend to accord a more hospitable reception to what they perceive to be the speaker's own thoughts than to the ideas of an unknown scribe.

Believability is the largest asset a speaker can project. Your own words, words that flow from your heart and brain, fall on more receptive ears. If you are believable, you can stumble, fumble (not too much, now, just a bit), and still finish with the feeling that your audience is nodding in agreement. Believability is more easily attained when you appear to be thinking for yourself rather than mouthing words like a ventriloquist's dummy. That is why speaking from notes—or without them— is better than reading from a prepared text.

In his abridged version of Plato's works, Henry L. Drake wrote of Plato: "He spoke without notes and recommended that few notes be taken because he thought that written words tend to escape the mind. It was his belief that repetition and meditation, rather than many notes, are the proper aids to memory."

There is little question that speaking without notes is the most powerful form of communication. You have full command of the audience. There is nothing to interfere with what you are saying. You are looking at the audience and they at you with no paper barriers. It is the most suitable medium for persuasion.

But it is also the riskiest.

Plato was right about repetition and meditation being the proper aids to sealing a speech in one's mind. Prerequisite is an exacting regimen, going over what you are going to say, again and again and again. I would also recommend *writing out the speech in full in advance.*

Don't trust to inspiration. Unless you are a consummate professional, trained and skilled by countless hours of speaking before numberless groups, inspiration will poop out on you when you need it most. I accept more speaking engagements than I should simply to keep my speaking skills honed. The more one speaks before audiences, the more professionally confident one becomes. And the obverse is also true: The less one speaks, the rustier one becomes.

John Connally has mastered with exquisite skill the no-notes speech. I have only a vague recollection of any time when I heard Connally speak from any kind of text. He is a formidable machine in action, the movie-star profile, the animal energy and silver hair adding to his dominant presence on the platform. I am convinced Connally does not write out his speeches in advance. Rather, he relies on a prodigious memory and an improvisatory technique that allows him literally to compose the greater part of what he is saying at the moment he says it. I do not recommend this course to anyone who is not thoroughly confident and considerably talented.

Another speaker whose assurance and courtly poise enables him to deal with complex, even abstruse, subjects without so much as a sliver of paper in front of him is Sol Linowitz, international lawyer and President Carter's special ambassador to the Middle East. I heard him speak for over twenty minutes explaining the Panama Canal Treaty (then the subject of a venomous congressional debate) with ease, lucidity, and the most precious quality of all, believability. It was a nonpareil performance, possible only from one with supreme belief in his (or her) ability to carry it off.

Another complete professional on a rostrum, without notes, is Ambassador Robert Strauss, former chairman of the Democratic National Committee. Indeed, Strauss is visibly less effective when he works from a written text than when he is winging it. Strauss's principal weapon is humor, Texas-bred, casually offered, and usually saucy, skittering along the borderline between what is just right and what is embarrassingly wrong. It is a testament to Strauss's skill on the stump that he invariably walks the edge of the precipice, but never falls off.

In September 1976, I made a speech to a gathering of some

2,500 people in Washington, D.C. The occasion was the first annual assembly of the National Italian American Foundation, an organization created in most part by the powerful and influential twenty-seven-person delegation of Italo-Americans in the Congress of the United States. The assembly was attended by the political heavyweights of the press, the Congress, the courts, the Cabinet, and the White House.

I was the principal speaker. Both President Gerald Ford and candidate Jimmy Carter were guests at the dinner, arriving and departing at differing times. Since Jimmy Carter arrived after President Ford had departed, he sat to my right as I delivered the speech without any paper in front of me. I remember that when I had finished he came up to me and his first words were: "How did you manage to give that speech without notes?" Before I could answer, he was caught up in the swell of the crowd.

For a specific purpose, I reproduce here the entire speech, as follows:

That most un-Italian of philosophers, Goethe, once wrote that to be happy one should each day look at a beautiful picture—read a beautiful poem—listen to beautiful music—and if possible say some reasonable thing.

Without realizing it, Goethe described the Italian spirit. If one believes in genetic linkage, then here in America, if you listen hard enough, you can hear the rush of two thousand years of Italian prose and poetry—of Italian song and laughter—and you can sniff the unduplicatable aroma of Italian brush and oil.

Tonight we are neither Republican nor Democrat, nor any other designation. What we are celebrating here tonight is not a political triumph or favorites at the ballot box or an election victory. We are lifted tonight by the tangible and beckoning instincts to which humankind has always directed itself—a soaring toward that which is higher and nobler and larger than the place where we began. That goal was mystically visible to Italian immigrants. It was sought and achieved: a full life by free people in a free and loving land.

The Italians came to this country in a great human flood at the turn of the century. Some five million arrived, mostly poor, mostly from the south, the Mezzogiorno. They came with pitifully small baggage, but with hearts bursting with desperate dreams. What they discovered at first was not that from which dreams are made. They found themselves aliens in a strange and bountiful land. But few turned back.

What they were looking for was not to be counted in dollars—or in earth they could aspire to. What they wanted was freedom to reach and grow—the possibility of something wider and worthier for their children and grandchildren—that was beyond their wildest imaginings in their bruised and barren homeland.

It may—it just may—be that what the Italians carried, not in their battered suitcases but in their veins and spirit, was precisely what Americans of all races and national origins seek so desperately to acquire. Today we are searching for values we have lost. We are looking for truths we have abandoned. We are nostalgic for traditions we have discarded.

The Italian contribution to America, though not contributed solely by them, was a veneration of those rediscovered assets which this society finds so luminous today: Passion for family—belief in church—affection for neighborhood—loyalty to friends—love of country. If there is an Italian heritage—precise—measurable—and splendid —it is those simple and lovely traditions.

They brought something else too. It is as alive and robust today as when those wide-eyed immigrants first arrived—clutching their few belongings—fearful but excited—ill at ease but fiercely determined. They brought a patriotic attachment to their new home that over two and three generations has neither slackened nor grown thin.

I remember my white-mustached grandfather, Sicilian, proud, dignified, dominant, speaking to me and his dozen grandchildren in heavy accents—thick with an odd mix of Sicily and the Texas Gulf Coast. "Love this country," he said. "Be proud of this country—it's a good land."

These were days before it was considered intellectually chic to shun visible affection for your country. My grandfather and his immigrant peers wouldn't have cared anyway. They were unashamed of their declared loyalty to their adopted nation. Their commitment was total.

The Italian immigrants of my grandfather's time were very much alike. Uneducated, with no knowledge of English, absolutely without possessions, they became part of the community in which they settled. They worked from sunup to darkness. They worked and saved and worked and invested. When they died, they owned a piece of America.

What they insisted on—and when the Italian patriarch insisted, it quickly became family dogma—was that their children and grandchildren be educated. These children would be taught no matter the cost—they would go to college no matter the sacrifice—they would learn no matter the hardship. And *then* they would be Americans—who cared deeply about the nation and *its* heritage.

And so the Italians in America learned—and laughed—and sang the songs of Puccini and Verdi. They argued with each other and drew the family close when tragedy and death invaded their homes. They went to great lengths to preserve the freedom they found. Some of them even went to Congress.

Now we are this day some twenty-six million, carrying

the Italian connection in our bones and blood. We are grateful for our ancestry. We are thankful for a journey taken a long time ago by our fathers and mothers, grandfathers and grandmothers.

No matter what destiny may demand of us, we will be as the Roman poet Horace wrote: "When a man is just and resolute, the whole world may fall and break upon him, and find him there standing in the ruins, undismayed."

I suppose that Jimmy Carter must have known I had memorized the speech, though I didn't deliver it precisely as I had written it.

This is the routine I followed:

First, the speech was broken into fifteen separate paragraphs. By dismantling the speech into paragraphs, you make the task of memory easier.

Paragraphing is particularly important in preparing a speech for memorization. Each paragraph should be short and should keep to one theme. Make the first sentence of each paragraph a key line that opens the door to the rest of what you wish to say, and make sure to have these key lines absolutely fixed in your mind. Then, even if you cannot remember all your words verbatim, you will be able to improvise from the theme of that opening sentence.

Second, I began by saying aloud, over and over again, the first two paragraphs. I did not worry that I did not say the speech exactly as it was written. But I strove to get the essence of the paragraphs settled firmly in my mind.

Third, after I had sufficiently committed the first two paragraphs to memory, I turned my attention to the next two paragraphs. Again the same routine: the speaking aloud of these two prose groupings until they were etched into my mind.

Fourth, then, for the first time, I put the first four paragraphs together and spoke them again and again.

Fifth, on to the next two paragraphs. I was by now into a disciplined groove of preparation. Within a short time I was able to speak with some confidence the first six paragraphs of the speech—almost half of it.

A strange thing happens as you go about this learning assignment. As you gain confidence in your ability to remember, the speed with which the work progresses picks up considerably. You begin to feel you are making measurable progress, and the effort to memorize is less drudging, and surely less daunting. Your exhilaration level rises rapidly.

Sixth, once I had finally put together the entire speech, I spent a good deal of time repeating it to myself. As I drove my car, instead of listening to the radio or dispatching my mind to some distant problem, I said the speech over and over again. In the shower and as I shaved, I repeated it. I usually kept a copy with me (not in the shower—the ink tends to run), so that if for some blighted moment my memory failed me, I could quickly glance at the written text to see what I had momentarily omitted.

Seventh, the day before I was scheduled to speak, I spent several hours with my stopwatch and my tape recorder, going over the speech for intonation and for timing. I made certain I would speak no longer than twenty minutes.

On the appointed evening, when I was introduced by Congressman Frank Annunzio of Illinois, I was totally and completely prepared. The hard work was behind me. The actual delivery of the speech was great fun for me, solely because I had prepared. Remember, when taking on an assignment like this, you must be committed to a regimen of preparation.

One final point: I personally believe that about 800 words is pretty much the outer limit for such an assignment in memorization. Anything longer requires more exhaustive preparation than most people are prepared to undertake.

I also believe that a 300-word or 400-word presentation ought never to be spoken from a prepared text. This length is about two double-spaced typewritten pages, or slightly less. If you are not capable (or, however mistakenly, think you are not capable) of committing to memory a talk of 300 to 400 words, then furnish yourself with some bare notes using key words and phrases from the final draft of your rehearsed speech.

All this is easy enough to do, *if* you are willing to work. The quality of your speech will diminish in exact proportion to the time you did *not* give to this special task of preparation.

When delivering a memorized speech, don't try to swallow the speech whole—it will give you indigestion. Rather, take the speech one paragraph at a time. Learn the first paragraph, go over it until you have it cold, then take on the second paragraph. Seal it in your memory, and then recap the first two paragraphs together. When you have those two indelibly in your mind, confront the third paragraph, and so on. Always repeat what you have memorized before you go on to a new paragraph. This is much the same advice that coaches and directors give to actors. Learn your lines piecemeal, enlarging what you have learned each time, so that eventually you will have captured in your memory cells what you need to say.

Obviously, one doesn't deliver speeches that require such intensive preparation every day. Such a schedule would exhaust anybody. I only make such speeches once or twice a year. Moreover, I did not give the speech in precisely the form in which I wrote it. Few speakers do. I used different phrasing and digressed slightly several times. But not so much as to unsettle my nerves; I persisted in holding on to the main thought—and my confidence. The prime element in such a speech is knowing the material so well that minor excursions outside the written text don't unhinge you.

The only two men I know personally who can produce that kind of speaking performance almost every time they rise to a rostrum are Louis Nizer, the famous courtroom attorney and author, and Ferdinand Marcos, President of the Philippines.

(There is a third speaker who can do the same, but whose real specialty—when he is not beguiling and mesmerizing a jury—is humorous storytelling. Edward Bennett Williams, on his feet, simply has no peer in engaging an audience, whether it is a packed hall or a dinner group. Warm, spirited humor and mimicry brought to a high art are the weaponry used by Williams.)

In December 1965, President Johnson sent a high-level delegation headed by Vice President Humphrey to the inauguration of Ferdinand Marcos as President of the Philippines. Ambassador Lloyd Hand, a Californian (but native Texan) and U.S. Chief of Protocol, and I also accompanied Humphrey.

Marcos, a compact, muscular man with heavy black hair and a flat-planed face, vaguely resembling Jack Palance, was during World War II the most heroic resistance fighter in those beleaguered islands. His exploits, legendary even among a host of legends, brought him a national affection that later propelled him to the highest office in that land. His fame as a fierce guerrilla fighter outshone in the public view his singular intellect and prodigious memory.

I sat beside Vice President Humphrey in the blaze of the noonday sun. We were perched on bleacher seats constructed some several hundred yards from the old Manila Hotel, a landmark in Luzon. More than fifty thousand Filipinos jammed the open space waiting to hear their new chief executive. Each of the various national delegations had been handed a copy of the President's address, printed on handsome paper and bound with a tasseled ribbon.

Marcos marched to a lectern bare of paper. He began to speak in Tagalog, the native language. After several minutes he switched to English, which he spoke in measured, slightly accented cadence, with his eyes directed at the mass of people. His voice was strong and, carried by the powerful loudspeakers studding the open area, boomed out for all to hear. Suddenly, it dawned on me that Marcos was speaking, word for word, what was printed in the pamphlet I was holding and reading. I nudged Humphrey and motioned to the text. Hubert's eyes lit up, for he, too, recognized what was being revealed to us: This man had memorized what later turned out to be over forty-five minutes of text. He was delivering it with passion and conviction, using chopping gestures to emphasize a point. His voice rose and fell, playing every note on the oratorical scale. It was an intellectual and emotional *tour de force,* a triumph of grand fluency.

His audience shrieked their approval, applauding, screaming, jumping in place. Marcos was composed, cool, as he turned to greet Humphrey, Hand, and me. Then he moved up and down the line of other dignitaries, smiling, totally in command.

It was, as I declared on later occasions, the single most effective speaking exhibition I ever witnessed, and for sheer professional skill it was an Academy Award performance. I cannot speculate how Marcos did it, though I ached to sit down with him and dissect the speech clinically, to observe his own preparatory routine.

In the intervening years I have heard Marcos speak on dozens of occasions with no diminishing of his skills. Each time, every element is in place, every note sounded musically, and the audience held captive by his spoken words. I have yet to see him use notes, much less a prepared text. His is one of those genetic rarities, a mind that can memorize—or at least put in polished form—whatever he chooses to say, and he can say it with loss of neither rhythm nor thought. Indeed, he forcibly captivates every audience.

Louis Nizer's technique, though similar to Marcos's in that they both eschew notes and texts, is more precise, more lawyerly (though Marcos is also a lawyer), more intellectual in his reach and poise. Nizer will seize a subject (what the world will be like in the year 2000, or the age-old quarrel between Israel and Arab nations, or the elusive definition of due process) and totally possess it. He has a beginning, a middle, and an end. He is a master of epigram, the whip-cracking phrase to illustrate a point ("When you point one accusing finger at someone, three of your own fingers point back to you"). He speaks in parable, always using the fable or aphorism or engaging phrase to illustrate the point he is making.

Williams uses the instrument of humor to keep his audience with him. Telling a story is a weapon often used by speakers of every hue and composition. But Williams's unduplicatable talent is the way his voice, like a brush, paints a whole palette of shadings and complexions.

Example: A prominent citizen is in deep trouble and hires a lawyer, named Bluzsky. Later the citizen comes to see Williams to hire him.

"But you have a lawyer, a good lawyer, named Bluzsky," says Williams.

"No," says the prominent figure, "I have fired him. I want you to take my case."

Williams goes over the file extensively, questions the prospective client at length, and finally says to him: "This is all very bad. The fact is you're guilty."

The fellow expostulates, "Hell yes, I'm guilty. If I was innocent, I would never have fired Bluzsky."

Picture the protean face of Williams, changing visage and

contour as he takes both parts in the story, and then see him rise in mock exasperation to shout, "If I was innocent, I would never have fired Bluzsky."

It is difficult for any audience (or jury) to remain aloof from Edward Bennett Williams.

Just before the Republican convention in 1952, in an interview with newsmen General Eisenhower disclosed some ideas about speaking in public, particularly in reference to memorizing speeches. The General said that Winston Churchill gave him "unshirted hell" for speaking from memory and not following the text of prepared remarks.

Even so, said the General, he did better without a text. "I'm through with prepared speeches, except in those cases where I have to have precise timing, such as radio and television." He said he would do things his own way, with reminder notes of the points he chose to make.

Eisenhower recounted how on one occasion in London, he had a 125-word message to deliver, so he memorized it and delivered it without a hitch. Churchill later reprimanded him severely. Said Churchill: "Never trust your memory in anything like that with people following every word you say to see if you repeated exactly what was written."

Churchill went on to advise Eisenhower to wear spectacles, "big round spectacles you can take off and shake in their face. And if you have notes don't try to hide them. Shake them in their faces, too."

Sir Winston, arguably the finest orator of his generation, always wrote out what he wanted to say, then transferred the written text to notes which he scrawled in his own hand or had typed after he had polished them to his satisfaction. This was his unvarying method of preparation, whether for a speech to be delivered in the Commons, an address to a large assembly, or a talk at a political gathering. No matter the locale or the occasion, Churchill laboriously composed his remarks and from the written text constructed his notes, which, as he advised Eisenhower, he brandished without shame to whatever audience he was addressing.

It may be that the one time Churchill did not follow his usual routine was when he returned as Prime Minister to speak to the students of Harrow, his boyhood school. When the Prime Minister was introduced, he rose to his feet, one hand tugging at his coat lapel, the other behind his back, and spoke the following words:

"Never give in. Never give in. Never give in, never, never, never—in nothing great or small, large or petty—never give in, except to conviction, honor, and good sense."

Whereupon the great man looked solemnly at his awestruck young audience, and sat down.

The fact is that though Churchill scolded General Eisenhower for his memory work on short speeches, the Prime Minister labored so long and so exhaustively over his important speeches that he did in fact memorize whole reams of prose and rarely consulted his notes. Unless, of course, the speech was long, loaded with facts that would be scrutinized later by those who had heard him, and set forth a policy declaration whose clarity he did not wish to cloud with any kind of imprecision.

Speaking from notes, particularly on a rostrum that is—at least to you—an important one, takes more than a modest amount of courage. You are, as it were, without the safety net of a written text. But it is an art that is, thankfully, easy to learn.

First, you must understand that preparation for such a speech is even more necessary than when you have a written text.

Second, don't let it worry you that you will probably never deliver a speech from notes the same way you have practiced it.

Third, essential to a successful notes-only speech is a firm grasp of the subject on which you are speaking.

If you are planning to speak only with notes to a convention of, say, investment bankers, and you are not an investment banker, have only a superficial knowledge of the subject, and know that once you dip beneath the surface of the subject you will be gasping for air—forget it. But if you are in the investment banking business, it is quite possible that you do know more than a little about your subject and can manage without a written text. Knowledge of the subject is the soundest armor one can wear.

The primary step is to set down on paper what you want to say. It is always useful to write the speech in full, so that you have before you all you intend to impart to the audience.

Then exercise as before: Read it over, again and again, until you have imprinted in your mind the core essentials of the speech.

Next, break the speech down into subject headings.

Put down in your notes any statistics you will need. If the numbers you will cite must be absolutely accurate, you ought to arm yourself in your notes. Any imprecision is likely to be remarked by your audience.

Keep in mind that speaking from notes requires your knowing your subject so well you can extemporize. Total command of your subject allows you to wander, as it were, because you can always find your way back to the central path from which you have strayed. To repeat the warning: Never try to speak merely from notes unless you know your subject cold.

Always try to commit to memory the last several sentences. The conclusion of a speech is one of its most important elements, often cementing all that you have said or, what is more usual, providing a graceful exit line that will summarize and make memorable what you have hoped to communicate. *Memorize* that last paragraph.

What follows now is a speech I delivered to the Union Society of Cambridge University in Great Britain in the fall of 1979. The Cambridge Union is the oldest of such university societies, a kind of debating forum where parliamentary leaders, professors, politicians from other lands, and people like myself who have had some experience in national government come to confront the students.

There is always a question-and-answer period afterwards.

The room itself is a replica of the British House of Commons, with chairs set on either side of the rostrum—actually a small table—on which sit duplicates of the dispatch boxes that reside on the real rostrum in the Commons. The audience sits, as do members of the Commons, in straight-backed chairs in rows perpendicular to the rostrum.

This speech was entitled "The Changing American Presidency."

Because I was the sole speaker this evening—for which I had crossed the Atlantic—and because the Union's program managers insisted, I designed this speech to run about thirty minutes, give or take a few minutes to extemporize and to extract a bit of humor from the moment.

The speech that follows is what I had written in advance, from which I drew my notes.

It was after midnight in the early weeks of 1966. President Johnson and I were sitting wearily on the second floor of the Mansion (the living quarters of the President and his family).

I was going over with him a pile of memoranda which needed his judgments before I moved them to the rest of the staff and the cabinet officers involved.

It had been an exhausting day, unusually so. The President had taken a ceaseless battering in the press, mostly on Vietnam, been vilified on the network news shows, been sliced up (happily in graceful prose) by *The Washington Post* and *The New York Times;* in brief, not a particularly exalting time in the life of the chief executive.

I looked at him curiously, sympathetically. His face was abnormally gray. He was tired.

"It strikes me, Mr. President," I said, "as damn strange why anybody would really want this job. Why should anyone have to submit to this kind of treatment."

The President smiled, the first time any kind of smile had crossed his face all day. "Well, Jack," he said, "if this job was easy, you wouldn't need a President. You could run the country with a part-time committee of shit-kickers."

The President's comment is a truth. More than any other element it makes visible the fascination of the presidency, the power of one man, that intrigues and mesmerizes all who contemplate it, the possibilities of triumph and applause, as well as equally spacious defeat.

Few of us are so seasoned in danger that we can, with calm repose, confront the political Grendels who threaten us. We are, subconsciously perhaps, eager for someone to lead us, defend us, command us, and eventually inform us that the danger has passed and we are for the moment secure.

Instinctively we are reaching out for an executive of clear eye and plain good sense who is called into service when the enemy's face is blurred, when we journey down unlighted passageways whose contour and formation are unknown to us. This kind of leader must, as Walter Bagehot put it: "Be concerned with far-seeing regulation of future conduct as well as limited management of the present."

In these sullen days he must explain, educate, soothe, make the dull understandable and the knotty seem ready to uncoil. Moreover, he must so inspire that when he summons the people to follow him to the mountaintop, they will do just that, even though they are not clear as to how hard the journey will be nor the view available to them when they arrive. If they arrive.

It is to such an enterprise that the American President will be called to command, and it is the equipment, physical, spiritual, and intellectual, he carries with him that will allow him, or not, to observe and understand how few are the alternatives he will be offered, and how meager the opportunities to enlarge them.

In the last fifteen years the modern U.S. presidency has changed radically.

The spur to that change (which is equally applicable to all Western democracies) is instant communications, the narrowing decision alternatives available to the chief executive, and the breakdown in discipline within and between the various parts of the government and the country. The deadly weaponry of war and the obscurities of economics have, together, distorted the lines of presidential persuasion, giving rise to a laxity in the reins of government. In short, being President in these times is tougher than it used to be. Responses once adequate and usable to a President are no longer sufficient.

The President must change the presidency because of:

a. Obscurity of the issues. There are no longer any readily identifiable archdemons presiding over easily recognizable barriers. There are no clearly defined targets. Now we are immersed in the bloated complexities of SALT II, inflation, snakes, floats, money velocity, monetary fluctuations, resource shortages, deficit balances of trade, interest rates, etc., none of which is easily comprehended and all of which require difficult sacrifices.

There is an instructive scene in a Robert Redford movie called *Three Days of the Condor* in which the veteran chief of the CIA, a spy pioneer with the OSS in World War II, discusses current problems with his young aide. The aide (Cliff Robertson) asks the old spy captain (played by John Houseman) if he has any nostalgia for the "good old days" of the late war. "Not really," replies the CIA director, "except I do miss the clarity."

b. Fragmentation and Balkanization of the Congress. There are no centers of congressional power anymore with whom a President can deal and negotiate, and then count on the leadership to deliver the votes required. Congress is fractured into subcommittees with a total breakdown in party loyalty, with maverick self-interest and constituency concerns in its place.

c. Instant communications. The collapse of restraints over what is and is not printed in the press and displayed on video is a spike in the heart of the presidency. We are dealing with an era of the abnormal presidency in which there is a "billy-club the leader" syndrome, where the game is to wound him, bleed him, and bring him down. Hedged in by what Mr. Churchill once called the "naggers and the snarlers," the President's expected tenure is now nasty, brutish, solitary, and short.

This is one reason why I, and others who have been intimate observers of the presidency, advocate a single six-year presidential term with no reelection eligibility.

d. A leakage of belief by the public in the ability of the government, particularly the President and the Congress, to make beneficent changes in the quality of their lives. The murder of a young President, the squalid behavior of the Nixon gang, the blight of Vietnam, the failure of old economic formulas in which we once had previously trusted, have all conspired to shatter the public's confidence in, as John Milton put it, "a government that is not beneath the reach of any point the human capacity can soar to."
e. The one durable asset that remains, curiously intact, and which no future President ought disturb or demean, is the lore, the mystique, the magic of the office.

What then is the major change in the conduct of the future presidency?

It is the role of the President as Educator-Communicator.

This means less emphasis on administrative roles and concentration on being teacher/inspirer of the public. The President has to select a few issues, the ones that cut to the bone of the nation, and concentrate on them, think hard about them, devise solutions. Then he must go to the people on television, again and again, to explain simply, lucidly, and possibly eloquently what the problem is, why it is important to the people, and what he needs them to do to help solve the problem. He leaves to his Cabinet officers the daily management of the government, under his stated policy. He concentrates on how to formulate solutions and how to communicate them to the people.

There are really only three basic issues that go to the heart of the future. They are:

1. The family pocketbook: The issues of food, housing, health, education, the stuff of daily living to which every family directs its attention and with which every family is rightly concerned. Unless the President presides over a robust economy, all else that he tries to do will fail. This is to say that if a President does his best, if he is admirable in his performance and in his efforts he makes to lift the quality of life in the nation, but cannot deliver what he has promised and what the people expect because the economy has faltered, he will be judged harshly. No adventure, domestic or foreign, can be proclaimed and acted on unless the President has taken care to build a solid economic base. It is the one element without which no President can lay claim to greatness.

2. The energy problem: The President must be prepared to put to hazard his political claims on the people's affections in order to design long-range energy production and conservation programs with definable and achievable goals. The time will surely come, unless Presidents in the future recognize the alien and unforgiving nature of bad judgment, when other countries swimming in hydrocarbons will submit the United States to blackmail unless we have in place alternative supplies of energy without which the nation's industrial armory will wither and die.

3. The achievement of an absence of war: He must do this in a widening ownership of nuclear weapons and the contagion of terrorism. But only a strong U.S. economy and a commitment of national resolve will give the President a place to stand.

These are the prime issues. All else are tracings on dry leaves in the wind.

But if the President is to accept the challenge of Educator-Communicator, he must have the ability to speak his cause believably with that mystical emotional rising through language, poise, and rhythm, without which he can only perform beneath greatness. With television really the only source of person-to-person communication between the leader and the people, the skill to lead is tied tightly to the ability to speak and inspire.

Therefore, the dominant role of the future President is that of teacher.

He must do what every great teacher does. He must gain our confidence so that we believe he knows what he is talking about. He must explain to us what it is he wants us to know, and do it in that special way that clears our mind, satisfies our curiosity, and depletes our suspicion. He must inspire us to follow him to the distant place where what he has conveyed to us has a meaning and a purpose. We must be ready to accept his summons and his reasoning even though we have no measure of what yet lies in store for us. It is that connection between people and President that is analogous to Walter Bagehot's description of Cabinet government in Great Britain, "the hyphen that joins, the buckle that fastens."

Is it then possible that, given the reshaping of the presidency, we in America can sort out our problems and find a way out of our current anxieties?

Can we repair the breakage of civic trust? Is it possible for a free and generous society to so manage its economic affairs that we are able to guarantee to every man and woman a choice of life course, to care deeply about those pressed to the wall because of circumstances beyond their control, and warrant, for all to witness, that the democratic strands that bind the Republic are not woven out of a defunct mythology?

I believe that the answer we are searching for is to be found in the national leadership of the President as Educator-Communicator. It is part of the myth-gathering property that belongs to the man, as Lord Macaulay said of young William Pitt, who thinks himself worthy of great things. "It springs," said Macaulay, "from a consciousness of great powers and great virtues and is never so conspicuously displayed as in the middle of difficulties and dangers which would unnerve and bow down any ordinary man."

Macaulay's design for leadership is what is required by the United States in the years ahead, so full of bitter choices to be faced. The future Presidents of our Republic have to understand the changing environment of their duties and to reshape their obligation to the people they have by solemn oath sworn to serve.

Reproduced on the next page are all the words on a paper I held in my hand, my notes from which the speech was delivered. Understand that the speech actually delivered was not an exact replica of the written speech that was passed to the press later. There were digressions, after which I tried to return to the text as best I could. I did not allow myself to be bothered by the fact that I was not delivering a precise duplicate of the written text. What I strained for was the essence of what I had prepared to say. Remember, your audience does not know when and where you are diverging. The essential element is to establish a rapport with the audience, to keep them interested in what you are saying. If their attention seems to be wandering, it is not the audience's fault but rather your own. Sometimes I injected a stab at humor to reclaim their attention and then, having fixed their interest on the point I was trying to make, went forward with the main thought.

You will see that the notes are signal lights, to direct my own concentration to the idea in each particular paragraph I spoke. Having read over what I wanted to say countless times, I was totally familiar with the essence of the written text, if not its actual wording. Each of the brief notes signaled to my mind the crucial parts of the idea or the phrase.

71

When speaking from notes, do not allow yourself to be thrown by the fact that you have not memorized your speech verbatim. Let the signal lights guide you. If you wander off the point, if you momentarily forget your original phrasing (which you thought to be delightfully designed) don't panic. Keep moving, and if the thought has fled your mind totally, go on to the next point, making as graceful a transition as you can muster. Keep in mind that the audience understands that you are speaking without the support of a full text and they will be tolerant—most of the time, that is. Keep looking at the audience, glancing at your notes only when you need to refresh your memory.

Here are my actual notes for the speech, "The Changing American Presidency."

Story of LBJ at midnight

President's comment a fixed truth

Few of us are so seasoned in danger . . . instinctively reaching out . . . (Bagehot)

In these sullen days . . .

It is to such an enterprise . . . few are alternatives offered, meager are opportunities to enlarge.

Presidency changed radically/spur to that change . . .

U.S. President will have to change the presidency.
1. Obscurity of the issues (THREE DAYS OF THE CONDOR)
2. Fragmentation/Balkanization of Congress
3. Instant communications

4. Leakage of belief by public . . . /durable asset remains

Role of President/Educator-Communicator

Three basic issues at heart of future.
1. Family pocketbook
2. Energy
3. Achieve absence of war

All else tracings dry leaves

Must have ability to speak eloquently

Role is teacher

Do what every great teacher does

Can repair breakage of civic trust?/democratic strands bind the Republic

Answer/Macaulay, myth-gathering property . . .

Conclusions: Macaulay's design for leadership is what is required by the U.S. in the years ahead, so full of bitter choices to be faced. The future Presidents of our Republic have to understand the changing environment of their duties and to reshape their obligation to the people they have by solemn oath sworn to serve.

Speaking from notes, particularly from a single sheet of paper, allows you to approach the rostrum virtually empty-handed, relieving your audience of the notion that the speech you are about to deliver will be an hour's agonizing embrace. There is, to an audience, something particularly welcome and gratifying in the sight of a single sheet of written notes.

And they will sense, as you speak, that what you say comes from the heart (a cliché to say that, yes, but in many ways true).

If you are a corporate officer talking to security analysts, or a city official addressing the Chamber of Commerce, the method of preparation is no different from that required by the treasurer of the local Rotary Club offering an accounting of the year's activities, or a housewife speaking to a citizens' group about a local legislative proposition.

The preparation of your material, the careful making of notes, the practice sessions you privately repeat—all these are the same no matter the ultimate environment of your speech. Speaking from notes is a learned craft, and anyone capable of sustained concentration and eager to make a good impression can do a good job with any audience.

Know your subject thoroughly. Write out the speech in full ahead of time. If you can't do that, at least write down the key points you want to cover and any figures you want to use. Put these down on paper in the order in which you want to deliver them. Write out your conclusion in full, and memorize it— then you will have the option of ending your speech at whatever point you consider it time to conclude, simply by using your closing paragraph.

A further word about eye contact: As you speak, you will find yourself gazing out at an audience—a blurred, indefinable mass. The fact that you are gazing but not seeing becomes readily apparent to those who are listening. Pick out several individual people. Speak directly to them. A woman in the front row: As you speak, talk directly to her. Lock your eyes on hers. After a moment or two, turn your head slowly to the other side. A balding man in a blue shirt: Fix your eyes on him as you talk.

The motive in this is quite simple. When you talk directly to a specific person, nervousness tends to fade, for you are now in a one-on-one conversation—which is ordinary. The incentive to shout or become strident is less. You are in a companionable situation, discussing your subject with someone who has come to hear what you have to say and is according you the compliment of sitting quietly while you talk. Moreover, you need not try to overpower, merely to persuade. You do this every day—in your family, in your business, as you shop and make inquiries.

The more you speak in public, the easier it will become to fasten your attention on one person and try to interest that person in what you are saying. After some practice, you will be pleasantly surprised to find you can discourse with more facility when your eyes are making friends with individual people in your audience. You will be able to move from one person to another, not abruptly but easily. It is the required first step in gaining rapport, a figurative handshake.

Put it another way: If you were in your living room conversing with a group of your friends and you gazed above them as you spoke, never meeting anyone's eyes, virtually talking over their heads, would you consider yourself impolite? Or arrogant? Would your friends be annoyed by your apparent rudeness?

Speaking to numbers of people in a more formal setting doesn't diminish the need for civility. Be interested in them as human beings, and not mere stage props conveyed to the hall for your exercise in public speaking.

Lord Chesterfield, a witty observer of mores and manners, summed up the necessity for winning over an audience. He once wrote: "The manner of your speaking is full as important as the matter, as more people have ears to be tickled than understanding to judge."

This is sound counsel.

Engage your audience by reaching out to them. As you speak, think that all who sit in front of you are your friends, with whom you will share something useful, valuable, or at least sufficiently attractive to absorb their attention for a few moments. If you are successful, you will have imparted a message that will be understood, retained, and even acted on.

V

THE COMIC LINE

When—and when not—to be funny

You walk near quicksand when you try to be funny. Uttering a comic line, telling a story that you hope will get a laugh, infusing wit into a serious subject: These are hazardous ventures for the speaker who is not by nature and inclination a humorous person.

The Earl of Louderdale, well known for his awkward ability to spoil any good story, once asked permission of celebrated Irish playwright Richard Brinsley Sheridan to repeat a funny story that Sheridan had recounted to a group of friends.

Sheridan replied: "My dear fellow, I must be careful of what I say in your presence, for a joke in your mouth is no laughing matter."

That anecdote contains the kernel of some very wise advice.

It is accepted dogma that one should begin a speech, any speech, with some kind of funny story. I recoil when I remember otherwise charming, sensible, and honest friends of mine who, on rising to discourse, begin by trying to regale their audience with a story calculated to loosen up the assembly. More often than not the story has little relevance to what follows, and it is usually presented with the skill one might expect of a butcher performing open heart surgery.

Humor is a delicate animal. When it is trotted out by anyone who in normal social intercourse is not noted for it, it becomes a shaggy beast hunkered down in the pathway of an otherwise sensible talk.

Even professionals stumble when they try to handle humor. John Lindsay, former mayor of New York City, is a man of immense electric charm. I admire him greatly. He is tall, handsome, with a roguish smile and a fine-timbred voice. Some years ago, before Lindsay had switched parties, he was selected to be the Republican speaker at the famous Washington Gridiron Dinner. Each year the senior members of the Washington press corps, who make up the membership of the Gridiron Club, choose a well-known Republican and Democrat to speak at their dinner. The format is unvarying: Skits throughout the evening satirize (sometimes with barbs dipped in curare) both parties' maladministration and bumbling. And the highlight is the introduction of the two selected speakers, whose presentations are supposed to be humorous—with a conclusion that is allowed to be serious.

The night before Lindsay's appearance, Art Buchwald held a small dinner party for his friend the mayor. Art Buchwald is one of those rarities, a genuinely funny man. He can recite portions of the Gospel according to Saint Mark and convulse his audience. He relies on a combination of speaking style and carefully formed prose tailored to his own unique personal gifts. He simply cannot be duplicated. Art had composed John Lindsay's speech for the Gridiron. At his pre-Gridiron dinner party, Art delivered Lindsay's speech. It was hilarious. All of us, veteran Washington observers, public officials, reporters, seasoned pros all, doubled over in laughter. The verdict was unanimous: "Lindsay will crock 'em tomorrow night."

The next evening, some 1,500 white-tied members of the Establishment—publishers from all over the country, government officials of high station, Supreme Court justices, political and business captains, congressmen, senators, ambassadors, White House aides, military brass, reporters, and the President and Vice President of the United States—were sitting chockablock in the Statler Hilton Hotel when John Lindsay rose to his feet.

I nudged a friend who sat next to me and whispered, "You're going to hear something that will put you in the aisles." My friend nodded appreciatively; he hadn't been in the aisles all evening.

Then John began to speak. He spoke well. The vowels were formed with grace. The sentences parsed. But the humor— where the hell was the humor? The lines that in Buchwald's mouth had driven us to helpless laughter the night before were now echoing hollowly through the hall with nary a chuckle. The singsong, undulating comic rhythms of Art Buchwald were replaced by the level patrician tones of the mayor. The exquisite Buchwald timing was nowhere to be found, the mayor substituting in its stead his own heretofore totally adequate St. Paul/Yale measured phrasing. Result: a large, fat, numbing bomb dropped by the otherwise splendidly charismatic chief executive of New York City.

The moral of the story is simply Sheridan's: What is hilarious from one person's mouth may be no laughing matter in another's.

Humor, however, is an attractive asset. Those of us who are not professional comedians should be able to learn how to repeat a comic tale.

Timing is the key to successful comedy. But achieving proper timing is the toughest task to complete. What you are aiming for is the abolition of stiffness and stuffiness. You are searching for an effortless manner—and a skillful handling of the punch line. Don't stumble over the punch line, or mouth it shabbily. And, if there are certain words that trigger the final effect, they should be carefully rehearsed, over and over again. A funny story should be practiced as diligently as an entire speech.

Let's take an example.

Say you are an accountant or an economist or a professor and you are speaking to a gathering of your own kind. You can tailor this story to fit your audience.

It could go something like this (if you are an accountant):

I am constantly reminded by those who use our services that we often turn out a ton of material on the subject but we do not always give our clients something of value.

A balloonist high above the earth found his balloon leaking and managed to land on the edge of a green pasture. He saw a man in a business suit approaching, and very happily said: "How good it is to see you. Could you tell me where I am?"

The well-dressed man replied: "You are standing in a wicker basket in the middle of a pasture."

(The story is told without trying to be an actor or a comedian. It is being told straight. Now you are nearing the punch line, so you must take care that you don't ruin the effect by stumbling over the next few words—no problem if you have prepared yourself.)

"Well," said the balloonist, "You must be a CPA."

The man was startled. "Yes, I am, but how did you know that?"

"That's easy," said the balloonist, "because the information you gave me was very accurate [now, a slight hesitation—a bare half-second] and absolutely useless."

This story isn't a belly-churner but it has several assets to give it bulk: It is relevant to the audience. It contains enough self-deprecating truth in it to be appreciated by the audience as not totally without foundation. And finally, it has a brief punch line.

It is the pause, the several-second hesitation between the speaking of one sentence and the beginning of another, that can become a speaker's high moment. The skillful use of the pause in a speech can, with practice, become as useful a tool as you can employ.

Remember Jack Benny's classic comedy routine in which he is approached by a mugger, who sticks a gun in his face and snarls, "Your money or your life."

Benny stands silent in his well-remembered pose, one hand under his chin, the other under his elbow.

The audience, well aware of his comic reputation as a cheapskate, begins to chuckle. Benny has not said a word. He merely stares. The laughter builds.

The mugger snarls again: "Did you hear what I said? Your money or your life."

And Benny, exasperated by the interruption, replies curtly: "I'm thinking it over!"

The laughter explodes.

Jack Benny was the master craftsman of the pause, the silence that can become an art form in itself.

Remember the pause: Just before you deliver a punch line, or, in a more serious vein, when you want to emphasize a concluding point or make a special impression on your audience . . . pause.

Though it might not mean much to Johnny Carson, appreciative laughter in response to a funny story has a magical, relaxing effect on a nonprofessional speaker. He or she has gained some minor rapport with the audience and, feeling a little more self-confident, will move into the meat of the speech with a touch more assertion than if the anecdote had, like a flightless dodo, refused to take off from the rostrum.

Adlai Stevenson wore the mantle of humor with more assurance and greater facility than almost any public man I have ever heard (with the possible exception of Hubert Humphrey).

I recall I once heard him speak in New Jersey to an overflowing crowd of high-powered businessmen, the loftiest industrial commanders of the nation, 99 percent of whom had gleefully voted against him twice and eagerly awaited a third chance to thumb him down.

Stevenson rose, cheery, paunchy, half-smiling.

His first words captured this hostile crowd.

"Mr. Chairman, I am grateful to be with you and to see in this audience so many of my friends [pregnant pause] —and none of my supporters!"

Laughter and then applause greeted the former presidential candidate, and the rest of the speech was hospitably received.

Humor is even more effective when it is encased within a speech, not as a separate story but as part of the fabric of the prose.

The late Senator Robert Kerr of Oklahoma was the master

of the throwaway line, huddled deep within a speech and leaping out when one least expected it.

He was speaking one day in Houston, Texas, and was describing a Republican opponent who had heaped invective on him during a campaign. "I don't mind being attacked but this fellow carried things too far. He was a very persuasive fellow. He could talk a dog off a meat wagon, but he was not very competent. His principal claim to fame was that he was once chief of police, but everybody in Oklahoma knew he was too dumb to fix a library card."

The audience of Texas oilmen was engulfed in laughter, and when the senator went on to advise them that the depletion allowance was a mighty good thing, they agreed. Enthusiastically.

Senator Kerr was also a master of the art of self-deprecatory humor. John Kennedy employed it as well, with grace and style.

When you aim to defuse an audience that may be hostile or when you are dealing with an issue—say, in a stockholders' meeting—that is likely to cause grumbling and disagreement among those to whom you are speaking, the use of self-deprecatory humor can be a soothing emollient.

On *Meet the Press* some years ago, Kerr was the guest to be queried by four newsmen, all of whom itched to get their hands on this super-wealthy oilman from Oklahoma. Kerr, like an old fox in a pasture he knew intimately, was mightily aware of the ambush. So, when the first question arose about his election in Oklahoma, he calmly evaded the ambush: "Waal," he said, "I just came off a tough and rough campaign. My opponent accused me of being a rich old oilman. And you know somethin'? He proved it on me!"

This was self-deprecation at its best. He had forestalled the sticky questions about to be hurled, had surprised a grin out of the hostile foursome, and from that moment on it was all plain sailing for the senator.

Shortly after his inauguration, President Kennedy addressed a hall full of press and congressmen at a large gathering in Washington. High on the list of mistakes and poor judgments the new young President was accused of was his selection of his brother Robert to be Attorney General when his legal and court experience was practically nil.

How did Kennedy deal with this matter? After a few quips to loosen up his audience, he turned to his brother, also on the rostrum, and said:

"There's been some criticism of me for selecting my brother to be Attorney General. I don't see anything wrong with my trying to give him some legal experience before he goes out to the private practice of law."

Whatever objections were souring the minds of those who listened, they were now mollified by this elegant self-deprecatory shot which, for the time, silenced the critics. Those close to the President observed, however, that the new Attorney General may have felt the humor was not so self-deprecatory, since the butt of the joke was Robert, not John. Nonetheless, the President knew precisely what he was doing, and what he did was eminently adequate to his needs.

Eppie Lederer, better known as Ann Landers, spoke to a group in Washington, seriously discussing modern assaults on the nerve ends of society—those concerns and fears that overwhelm all families, including the prospect of crime in the streets. In the middle of her recitation of dismal statistics Mrs. Lederer paused. "The fact is," she deadpanned, "that in Washington it takes steel nerves to be a neurotic."

The juxtaposition of uncongenial truth with a creative comic line brought the audience alive. It made the acceptance of surly fact a bit more appealing.

* * *

Often there is opportunity to rise at a dinner party and toast the honor guest. In Washington the after-dinner toast is something of a tribal rite, as much a part of the dinner gathering as the cocktail and the soufflé. Dinner toasts have only one unvarying rule: brevity.

When Henry Kissinger was the National Security Advisor to the President, before he ascended to the seventh floor of the State Department as Secretary of State, he hosted the Chinese ambassador to the United States in the first flushed days of Sino-American reconciliation. The dinner took place at the fashionable Bistro Restaurant in Beverly Hills. The great of Hollywood were present, as well as a cadre of Chinese officials, only one of whom spoke English. This gentleman was seated just behind the ambassador, whispering into his ear the arcane speech of the American guests.

Among the famous movie stars at the table was Kirk Douglas. When Kirk rose to honor his host, he had the mischievous thought of testing the resourcefulness of the interpreter with a one-line toast. He smiled widely, lifted his glass, looked firmly at the ambassador, and said: "I lift my glass to Henry Kissinger, who is as American as apple strudel."

The Chinese ambassador cocked his eye toward his link with the English language, but alas, the interpreter gulped, hesitated, and then poured a torrent of words into the weary ear of his chief. The ambassador nodded briefly, turned to look at his aide, who murmured again, then turned back to Kirk and nodded appreciatively.

Kirk later said to me, "I always wondered what the hell that interpreter said to the ambassador."

Kirk had spoken briefly, and he had said enough to lengthen his one sentence in English into a thousand words of Chinese. Damned inscrutable, these Americans.

Sometimes you have to be careful about humor. It should not offend those to whom you speak. For example, I am not sure I didn't go a little overboard one evening when I was speaking to a group of cruise-ship operators. After heralding the fact that cruise-ship vacations were big business (to which they nodded appreciatively) and citing other facts well known to them, I casually injected, "But as for me, I heartily dislike sea travel. Not only is being on a ship like being in prison, but there is the added possibility that you may drown."

A slight hesitation as the audience pondered that a few seconds, then steadily rising laughter. I did not inform them of the further truth that I had stolen the line, with minimal alterations, from Dr. Samuel Johnson—I didn't want to burden them with too many footnotes.

The best humor is spontaneous humor, not storytelling or gags, but humor derived from the material of the speech or built on something that has been said or done on the occasion of the speech.

This means you should listen carefully to all that has been said before you rise to speak. Drawing humor from the moment is a fine art, but it can be learned if you listen attentively. You can't tell ahead of time what you may be able to draw from previous speakers, but often it can be a crucial part of what you say later.

Here is one example:

Some two years ago, I was asked to be the speaker at the annual banquet staged by Covington & Burling, Washington's largest and most prestigious law firm. Two hundred or so lawyers and their spouses and friends gathered to enjoy themselves (and in a big firm like Covington & Burling, some are meeting each other for the first time!). It is an evening in which the speaker, if he is to survive the next day's comments, strives to avoid being long-winded and blowsy. Not being a lawyer, I had nothing technical to convey except some observations about Washington itself.

I was introduced by a brilliant young partner of the firm,

Coleman Hicks, a Yale Law School graduate. In his introductory remarks, Hicks was slyly amusing, offering some in-house jokes about his associates which drew appreciative chuckles from his audience. I listened intently to his presentation.

When my turn came I rose and began:

"I am not sure I can follow the humorous sallies constructed by Coleman Hicks. Anticipating such a prelude, I consulted with my friend Art Buchwald. He reassured me. 'Jack,' he said, 'just remember one thing: There is no such thing as a Yale lawyer with humor. Odd, maybe; strange, perhaps; rich, always; but humorous, no.'"

The audience seemed to love it, including the Yale Law School alumni. Some of them even managed a tight, thin slice of a smile.

In the spring of 1981, I was one of several on a rostrum before a large assembly of Washingtonians gathered to "roast" Art Buchwald. Also scheduled to speak were Irving Lazar, the famous literary agent; Philip Geyelin, syndicated columnist for *The Washington Post;* George Stevens, Jr., co-chairman of the American Film Institute and son of the distinguished movie director; and Joseph Califano, the former Secretary of Health, Education and Welfare, who some months before had been unceremoniously sacked by President Carter.

Mr. Califano made a delightful talk toasting and roasting Art, except that he inadvertently used a line I was myself poised to deliver.

When I was introduced, before I launched into my own diatribe I greeted the audience and then turned to Califano: "I am a bit vexed because Joe Califano just stole one of my best lines. Now I know why President Carter fired the 'sumbitch.'"

The crowd roared in appreciative laughter. Because I had listened to Califano, I had been able to forge a fairly good riposte —which the audience knew had not been in my mind when the program began.

Use the time before you are called on to speak to open your ears and *listen.* There is almost always something said or done in those moments that you can utilize to spark your presentation, to give it immediacy—most assuredly a sharp arrow to fit to your bow.

Humor is also more appreciated when it is least expected.

In the summer of 1981, at Twentieth Century-Fox studios, a reception was held for Arlene (Mrs. Alan) Alda. Arlene is a bright, charming lady who with unique confidence bears the burden of being the wife of a celebrated movie and television star. She is seldom before the public, since her principal task has been that of wife and mother of three daughters. But on this evening there was a jubilant celebration of the publication of her new book, entitled *On Set* and containing photographs she had taken of the making of her husband's latest film, *The Four Seasons.* She wrote the text also, sure-handed prose about the inside of movie making.

Arlene was introduced by Dennis Stanfill, at the time the chief executive of the studio. She came to the microphone: a small, smiling, obviously happy lady.

The audience expected a serviceable few words, and was ready to applaud civilly and appreciatively. The food had been delicious and there were celebrities present to satisfy the stargazers.

She began:

"I am not very good before an audience. I usually leave that to my husband. Indeed, I was quite nervous when I appeared on the *Today* show to be interviewed by Tom Brokaw. I sat in the Green Room. [*Note:* This is the room where guests await their turn to appear on a show and from which they are summoned by an assistant producer.] A young lady came in with a clipboard, bustling with energy and some hesitation. She came up to me and said: 'Are you the person who is against spanking?' I said, 'No, but I would be glad to sign the petition.' "

The audience, surprised by the sudden splash of humor, exploded into laughter.

But she wasn't through:

"I am always asked how it feels to be Mrs. Alan Alda, wife of a famous director, writer, star, and sex symbol! After the tour we put together all my answers to this question, asked about a hundred times, and the result of the compilation was that I was a pathological liar."

Again, the audience screamed its delight.

And then:

"On tour we stopped in Denver and dined with Marvin and Barbara Davis. [*Note:* A week earlier, Mr. Davis, a Denver oil billionaire, had purchased Twentieth Century-Fox.] When I told the Davises of the some thirty or forty cities on my itinerary, Barbara Davis looked at me curiously and said: 'Who's going to do your hair?' "

After this, it was the settled conclusion of the assembly that Arlene was the star of the Alda family. Her speech was totally professional, totally relevant, and quite unexpected.

One wouldn't describe the late Nikita Khrushchev as one of the great humorists, but he possessed a cunning peasant wit dug out of the ancient soil of Mother Russia herself. John Roche, former LBJ White House aide, now a Tufts University professor and syndicated columnist, once wrote about Khrushchev's famous 1966 secret speech. This address to the Supreme Soviet contained a stunning compilation of Stalin's brutal crimes, and marked the first time anyone in the Politburo had the temerity to go public with that lamentable catalogue. After Khrushchev had finished he responded to questions, all of them written out on paper and handed up to the speaker.

One question was, "Since you knew Stalin was a monster, why did you work so closely with him?"

Khrushchev read the question and, without a moment's hesitation, replied, "For the same reason the comrade who sent up this question did not sign it."

Mr. Roche does not describe the reaction of the audience.

It is one thing to plan one's sallies in advance; it is quite another to fling a piece of barbed prose even as the oratorical muskets are firing. In my judgment perhaps the finest example of spontaneous wit is the instant response of Harold Wilson, former Prime Minister of Great Britain but at the time leader of the Labour Opposition, in a debate in the Commons.

Duncan Sandys, the Tory Minister of Defence (and Churchill's son-in-law), had just spoken on the subject of the Blue Streak missile which was apparently unable to get off the ground but still was part of the British defense arsenal. When Sandys had completed his rebuttal to critics of the Blue Streak, Wilson rose quickly to his feet, one hand grasping his coat lapel.

"We all know," he began, "why Blue Streak was kept on although it was an obvious failure. It was to save the Minister of Defence's face. We are, in fact, looking at the most expensive face in history. Helen of Troy's face, it is true, may only have launched a thousand ships, but at least they were operational!"

Sandys could find no suitable rejoinder.

Sir Winston Churchill was an admitted master of the literate karate chop. In a debate with Austen Chamberlain, half brother of Neville Chamberlain (Britain's Prime Minister at the infamous Munich meeting with Hitler), Churchill looked squarely at Chamberlain and said in mock sorrow, "The honorable gentleman has always played the game [a slight pause] and has always lost it."

It was the same Churchill who devastated the monkish Sir Stafford Cripps with one sentence: "He has all the virtues I dislike and none of the vices I admire."

Humor readily at hand was reported by writers in the ancient classics. Alcibiades was telling Pericles how Athens should be governed and Pericles was more than a little irritated at the young lad's effrontery.

"Alcibiades," the great Pericles admonished him, "when I was your age, I talked just about the way you are now talking." Whereupon Alcibiades smiled and retorted, "How I would have enjoyed knowing you, Pericles, when you were at your best."

Thomas Reed, the famed Czar Reed, Speaker of the House at the turn of the century, once listened to Theodore Roosevelt expound at length on some subject in which Roosevelt made it patently clear that he was both expert and right.

Reed wearily lifted himself to his feet and said, "Theodore, if there is one thing more than another for which I admire you, it is your original discovery of the Ten Commandments."

It has been written (and while this response may be apocryphal, I yearn to believe it is true) that Voltaire was approached by a minor historian whose latest book Voltaire was prevailed upon to read through the importunings of intermediaries. When the historian chided Voltaire for his failure to comment, Voltaire quickly replied: "A historian has many duties. Allow me to remind you of two of which are important. The first is not to slander, the second is not to bore. I can excuse you for neglect of the first because few will read your work. However, I cannot forgive you the second, for I was forced to read what you had written."

If I had a choice, I would have enjoyed listening to John

Randolph of Roanoke, who was President Thomas Jefferson's floor leader in the House of Representatives, later senator from Virginia, and a cobra-tongued orator whose vituperative wit caused other public men to shrink from his encounter in debate. He brought malice to its most poisonous levels and did it with a wit unequaled by any other parliamentarian in the early days of the Republic.

A brave but inadequate lancer who rose to joust with Randolph was a certain Philomen Beecher, congressman from Ohio. Randolph tolerated for a while Beecher's interruptions of "Previous question, Mr. Speaker," but when this had happened a number of times, Randolph finally turned a baleful glance on the noisy member.

"Mr. Speaker," Randolph said, "in the Netherlands, a man of small capacity, with bits of wood and leather, will in a few minutes construct a toy that will, with the pressure of a finger and thumb, cry 'Cuckoo, cuckoo!' With less ingenuity, and with inferior material, the people of Ohio have made a toy that will, without much pressure, say 'Previous question, Mr. Speaker!' "

Amid gales of congressional laughter, Philomen Beecher slunk out of the chamber and out of history.

There is a contemporary sound to Randolph's wit. In a debate over an expensive appropriations bill, Randolph spoke in favor of economy, and ended his remarks (all without notes, I must add) with this shot: "That most delicious of all privileges . . . spending other people's money."

As the senator from Virginia, Randolph listened to Missouri Senator Thomas Hart Benton's filibuster for four solid days. When the filibuster had ended, Randolph rose and commented dryly: "I must remind my colleagues that Senator Benton's speech lasted one day longer than the French Revolution of 1830."

The melding of brain and tongue was so swift in Randolph that no one could be certain of his retort nor how lethal would be its explosion. He peppered two members of the House with one shot when he said about Robert Wright and John Rea (pronounced "Ray") that the House of Representatives contained two curious juxtapositions: "A Wright always wrong and a Rea without light."

One time a new member came to the House, elected to fill out the term of a dear friend of Randolph's who had died suddenly. The new member immediately began, with more courage than good sense, to cut up Randolph on the House floor. Randolph bided his time, until one afternoon discussion turned to a bill in which Randolph's late friend had had a keen interest.

Said Randolph gravely, ". . . this bill has lost much in the death of my dear friend, whose seat, alas, still remains vacant."

Before Martin Van Buren became President, he crossed Randolph in debate. The Virginian arose from his seat to comment on Van Buren: "He is a man who habitually rows to his object with muffled oars."

The largest talents of the Congress were not immune to Randolph's peculiar moods. He considered John Calhoun a man mad with lust for war. He never forgave or forgot Calhoun's stand as one of the war hawks who pushed the United States into the War of 1812, which Randolph opposed with all the fervor he could summon—and that was quite a lot.

When Calhoun was Vice President under John Quincy Adams, Randolph once began a speech in the Senate with these words: "Mr. Speaker, I mean Mr. President of the Senate and would-be President of the United States, which God in His infinite mercy avert."

Nonplussed, Calhoun was struck with silence, which was, by historical precedent, the proper way to confront Randolph.

In the history of speechmaking, there is one grand master, Benjamin Disraeli, who late in his life (at age sixty-three for one year, and then again at seventy) became Prime Minister of

England. (The following is extracted from *The Bitter Taste of Glory*, a book I wrote about great political leaders):

On the floor of the Commons, Disraeli was master. He was a professional, totally in charge of the complex procedures of the House, and instantly knowledgeable of the labyrinth of debate. He battled all the great orators of the day, unattended by aides or colleagues, with either his skill or his courage, never faltering even in ill-health, always feared, often hated, never ignored.

Early in his career, he took on Sir Robert Peel and destroyed him. It was done deftly, precisely, and with a surgeon's unerring eye for the right place to apply the scalpel.

It began rather inauspiciously. Peel rose to cut down this foppish young innocent. He used as his saber some lines uttered by a predecessor, Canning. The lines were apt and effective. But it was a dangerous game that Peel played, for he had done to Canning exactly what Canning's lines had reproved.

These are Canning's words, quoted by Peel:

> *Give me the avowed, the erect, the manly foe,*
> *Bold I can meet—perhaps may turn his blow!*
> *But of all plagues, good Heaven, thy wrath can send,*
> *Save, save, oh save me from the candid friend!*

Disraeli did not reply at first. A few days went by. Then Disraeli spoke quietly, to protest against the system of appealing to the loyalty of the Tories in order to make them vote for Whig measures.

It is valuable to give Disraeli's reply, for no one can capture the luxuriant shatter of the retort without the actual words. Listen to Disraeli:

The right honourable gentleman [Peel] caught the

Whigs bathing and walked away with their clothes. He has left them in the full enjoyment of their liberal position and he is himself a strict conservative of their garments. [The House laughed uproariously. Peel sat somber.]

If the right honourable gentleman may find it sometimes convenient to reprove a supporter on his right flank, perhaps we deserve it. I for one am quite prepared to bow to the rod, but really, if the right honourable gentleman, instead of having recourse to obloquy, would only stick to quotation, he may rely on it, it would be a safer weapon. It is one he always wields with the hand of a master; and when he does appeal to any authority, in prose or verse, he is sure to be successful, partly because he never quotes a passage that has not previously received the meed of parliamentary approbation, and partly and principally because his quotations are so happy.

The right honourable gentleman knows what the introduction of a great name does in debate—how important are its effects and occasionally how electrical. He never refers to any author who is not great and sometimes who is not loved, Canning for example. That is a name never to be mentioned I am sure in the House of Commons without emotion. We all admire his genius. We all, at least most of us, deplore his untimely end. And we all sympathize with him in his fierce struggle with supreme prejudice and sublime mediocrity—with inveterate foes and with candid friends. The right honourable gentleman may be sure that a quotation from such an authority will always tell. Some lines, for example, upon friendship written by Mr. Canning and quoted by the right honourable gentleman. The theme, the poet, the speaker—what a felicitous combination! Its effect in debate must be overwhelming; and I am sure, if it were addressed to me, all that would remain would be for me thus publicly to congratulate the right honourable gentleman not only on his ready memory, but on his courageous conscience.

The House was in an uproar. It was a stunning achievement. Peel sat hunched in his seat, quiet, breathing heavily, deeply provoked, but determined not to reveal it, and deeply hurt, hurt beyond measure that this upstart should be so savage, so gaily malignant to the Prime Minister.

Some time later he attacked Peel again, even more cruelly. He spoke with telling effect, and the last twenty minutes of his speech were rapid-fire shots of invective and deadly sarcasm.

He described how the Peelites, "like the Saxons confronting Charlemagne were converted in battalions and baptized in platoons." He hit Peel savagely for his vacancy of mind and his use of other people's ideas. "His life has been one long appropriation clause. He is a burglar of others' intellect. There is no statesman who has committed political larceny on so large a scale." It was the most cruelly discomforting day of Peel's career. One month later, he was thrown out of office. Disraeli had pulled the great man down.

We are more polite today, at least in the clubby atmosphere of the cloakroom, the stump, and the TV studio. But the absence of ceremonial verbal assault may be due more to the diminution of the art of lethal reply than concern for the other fellow's feeling. The format of opposition today has been drained of any style. It is mostly formless, noisy, rowdy, and, if a good phrase has surfaced, it has gotten lost in the cluttered din from which it came.

Pilfering is socially acceptable among speakers. Stealing

good stories from those who are rich in the creative gift of laughter is an unpunishable, even fashionable, oratorical felony.

The irrepressible John Randolph, whose wit we have already examined, was the source of a bit of borrowing by a twentieth-century member of the U.S. Senate.

Once Randolph bore in on a hapless colleague with the statement: "His mind is like a parcel of land, poor to begin with and rendered more barren by too intensive cultivation."

That nugget lay glistening but unnoticed in the *Congressional Record* for a long time. Then in 1919, almost ninety years after Randolph died, Senator Thaddeus Caraway of Arkansas stood on the Senate floor to bang away at the patrician senator from Massachusetts Henry Cabot Lodge: "I have long heard of the reputation for wisdom and wit of the senator from Massachusetts, but his speech today has convinced me that his mind is like the land of his native state, barren by nature and impoverished by cultivation."

There were many that day who were astonished at the spontaneous wit of Senator Caraway. Few of them knew that somewhere in the recesses of Caraway's mind was that classic Randolph line, which he had no doubt read and retained to skewer Henry Cabot Lodge. Ah, to possess the "spontaneous" retort!

If you find yourself speaking in public several times a year—in business or in conferences or at conventions or your community service club—begin to keep a journal of lines, sentences, stories, retorts you have read or heard. You will find this a treasure trove when you have to rise to your feet. Oftentimes, as you gain more assurance through practice, you will find one of these proven "bell-ringers" (as an old professional speaker once termed them) springing out of your memory, and you can toss it off as if you had coined it on the spot.

I keep a journal and have done so for many years. Every time I find a line or two that I value in a book I underline it and later write it in my journal. Over the years I have accumulated a fat volume of over three hundred pages brimming over with words I have appreciated—stately lines from great authors, sprightly humor from antic wits. When I inscribe a quotation in my journal, I carefully note where I heard or read it, and from whom. If the item is from a book, I include the author, the title of the book from which it came, and the page number, so I can always refer back to the original to see the context in which it was said or written.

Disregard books of quotations. Too often a quotation from Bartlett's sounds exactly as if you had lifted it. It lacks the verisimilitude of the original, and besides, I count ransacking a quotation book a form of cheating. If I haven't read it in a book or heard it from a speaker, I consider its use equivalent to peeking at the hidden cards in solitaire.

You will find a detailed, alphabetized personal journal or card index of memorable phrases quite helpful in adding a light touch to your written speeches. An apt line will spark your creative juices, allowing you to refine, rephrase, redesign the words to fit your specific audience and occasion.

VI

THE CAMERA EYE

How to speak before television cameras

To say that television has transformed the art of speaking is to utter the cliché of the generation.

In a workaday world grown complicated, so choked with technological alternatives and head-splitting econometric riddles, no one who aspires to success in any profession can neglect the art of communication. The role of communicator has become dominant in the careers of businessmen, professors, union shop foremen, politicians—of anyone who must try to convince others of a point of view. Even when your forum is a PTA meeting or a club where policy is being discussed, you are more apt to be persuasive if you understand something about the delicate art of speaking to others.

It is not enough to be intellectual, gorged with facts, smart, competent in administration or in designing strategy. You must be able to speak reasonably, believably, engagingly to those whose support is necessary to your cause.

Knowing all the facts is one thing. Imparting those facts to others so that they understand and are open to persuasion is quite another. When knowledge is disjoined from the communication of knowledge, one may as well be shouting to the wind.

In these days, perhaps the principal medium for the communication of knowledge is television. Sooner or later in your life, the cameras may well be on you. There is no surer charm you can carry than the ability to say easily and clearly what you believe and why you believe it.

But you must bear in mind that speaking before a television camera is not the same as speaking to an audience in a large room, an auditorium, a sports arena, whatever. It is totally different. Unless the speaker understands that difference, the quality of speaking suffers.

Television is intimate, almost as if those who watch and listen are seeing you through a microscope. Vocal inflections, facial expressions, even the color of your tongue and alignment of your teeth are magnified and intensified.

The indispensable element of television speaking: Be conversational, as if you were in a living room talking to a half-dozen people. This does not mean you cannot gesture or lift your voice on a declamatory note, but it does mean you need not raise your voice too many decibels in order to be heard. Your very whisper becomes gloriously (or otherwise) audible.

Try to keep your passions in check, for what in a large auditorium is reasonable can become on TV wildly ridiculous, even grotesque. I am reminded of Moliere's thought that while men do not get upset over being called wicked, they do strenuously object to being made ridiculous.

Often nonprofessionals (even, alas, professionals) are so mesmerized by the all-engulfing eye of the camera that they lose touch with reality.

Try to forget the camera eye. In fact, one *must* forget the camera eye. If you don't, sooner or later your tongue and mind will collide. Not a happy prospect.

There are several ways to keep the camera eye from distracting you. If you are on a panel show, or having a conversation with a group, or in a one-on-one interview, concentrate on those to whom you are talking. Look them in the eye and speak as if you were chatting in your home.

If you are speaking alone in a studio, it helps if some of your friends stand near the camera so you can speak to them. If no one is available, then imagine the camera eye to be a window through which you are speaking to the cameraman on the other side of the lens.

The key is to consider the camera as anything but a camera. Conceive it as a window or a two-way mirror, or pretend that someone you trust is sitting in front of you. Speak to that imaginary friend.

Whenever you are in a television studio facing the camera, there is usually some delay, interminable to anyone anxious and nervous, before you get the signal to begin. These are crucial seconds. Your throat may grow dry. You may even find yourself having difficulty swallowing. It happens to the hardiest professionals. One reason for it is the distraction of that impersonal round black eye of the camera, focused so steadily on you. It is a most discomfiting gaze.

That is why I think it useful to have someone (preferably

two or three people), either friends of yours or studio techni-
cians, stand slightly behind and around the camera. When
your cue comes, and the red light that signals the "on" camera
adds its baleful glow to the lens's eye, talk to them. If they are
grouped closely around the camera, you will not be diverting
your own gaze too far to the left or right of the lens but will
be able to talk to living people rather than that robotlike, sterile
companion.

I tried, endlessly and without success, to persuade President
Johnson, when delivering a television speech from the Oval
Office, always to seat a couple of his friends or his family
cheek-by-jowl with the camera. "Talk to them, Mr. President,
not the camera. Let the camera eavesdrop on what you are
saying, but speak directly to those seated next to the camera."
LBJ did it *his* way.

But in truth, the camera viewed merely as eavesdropper
becomes a lesser intrusion, a kind of bystander. It is so very
much easier to speak naturally, warmly, even passionately, to
folks you know than to that unblinking, bloodless Cyclops.

Don't panic if you feel an explosive anxiety just before you
begin to talk. It is natural, and human. Keep in mind that you
will be talking conversationally to people. Look them in the
eye, not the camera.

Again, preparation is the companion of success in any kind
of TV speaking.

Know what you want to say. Don't worry about remembering precise phrasing, but know essentially the ideas you want
to present. This means prior study. Think about what you will
say at some length beforehand. When you are by yourself you
might even speak aloud what you intend to say, always
remembering that you probably will say it differently when
you are before the camera. That is not important. Don't let
memory frighten you—you don't have to memorize. Know the
outline of what you intend to say. Sometimes, if there is suffi-

cient advance notice, you can have a TelePrompTer beneath the camera lens to offer the security of the printed word to fall back on.

If you are on a question-and-answer show where others are going to query you, "moot court" your appearance. That is, do as lawyers do before they try a case, or as Presidents of the United States do before appearing at a press conference: Try to figure out in advance the questions you think you will be asked. If the format of the program is known, it is a simple proposition to predict almost all the questions that will be put to you.

Before each press conference, President Johnson would sit with his advisers for several hours. We would assume the roles of reporters and ask the most savage questions we could construct. We would go over, time and time again, those questions which our intelligence-gathering told us would most likely be posed. We would ask the questions in snarling tones, trying to duplicate, insofar as it was possible, the actual press conference to come.

After each question, the President would answer. Then we would explore and dissect his reply. Not quite right. Not really to the point. Then, the question again.

What about a question that the President really didn't want to answer, or that required him to reveal so much about his intentions or strategy that he would be boxed in, unable to make alternative moves? The solution would be to "fuzz up" the answer so that he could glide out of that minefield and land lightly on another query more easily handled. "Fuzzing up" doesn't mean lying, or even dancing around the turns, but simply keeping one's options open. We concentrated on these questions until the President was satisfied that his answer was pointed enough but not sufficiently revealing to impede his future actions.

To be honest, this kind of hazy response did invite disaster.

Often what we considered a reasonable answer didn't take with the press.

On one occasion, we knew the President would be asked about the removal of Henry Cabot Lodge as ambassador to Vietnam. The President had earlier determined that Lodge would be brought back and he had already asked General Maxwell Taylor to take his place. Taylor had agreed, and it was only a matter of waiting for the appropriate time to make the announcement. But Lodge had not yet been informed specifically, so it was agreed by all that this particular press conference was not the time to light that torch. How to maneuver? How to field the question we knew with absolute certainty would be asked?

The exchange went something like this:

Question: "Mr. President, are you thinking about removing Ambassador Lodge and are you thinking now about a successor?

The President without breaking stride answered, "No, I am not thinking about that at all. Next question."

Consider the Jesuitical logic of that answer, and the way it was asked. "Are you thinking about . . . ?" The President's answer to him was totally correct and to him totally honest: No he wasn't thinking about that at all. He had already done it, so he wasn't thinking about it!

Several days later when the President did make the announcement, the press landed on him with bludgeons and meat axes. Credibility gap! President untruthful! Goddamn lie! These were some of the milder aspersions.

The President was genuinely upset. How on earth could he be libeled as being untruthful, when in fact he had answered honestly and correctly? He was *not* thinking about it.

The White House staff gulped a few times, and we had to admit as we sat around grousing about press conspiracies that the press did have a point. But how else to handle it? That was a no-win situation, and we were armed with a feebly righteous sword which we brandished without much effect.

Television has reshaped the language and the rhythms of speech. Because time is so important in TV, thirty to forty seconds becomes a long time for one person to be on camera.

Seasoned professionals in public life learn early that when a newsman sticks a microphone in front of your face the first priority is to be brief. The second priority is to say what you want to say, and wish to have heard by the audience, in one to three sentences. The third priority is to try to give what you say some color.

Why these precautions? On network and local news shows, there is more material than can be used. It is the role of the editor to cull out the banal, the droning, the bulky, the inadequate, and to keep intact what is useful to the story and, importantly, adds sauce (whether laughter, sympathy, anger, grief, or other emotional component) to the segment.

Therefore, if what you say is succinct and has heft, the chances are you will not end up on the cutting-room floor.

When the fifty-two American hostages returned from their imprisonment in 1981, one of the group who was particularly articulate on television was Bruce German. He was, by instinct, brief and pungent in expression. "Would you go back to Iran?" he was asked.

Without breaking stride, he answered "Yeah, in a B-52."

That segment of film hit every network and local news show. It was simply too good to be edited out.

* * *

I persistently advise my congressional friends to keep in mind a simple admonition. When a senator or congressman leaves a committee hearing or a visit with the White House staff or whatever, he should head for the waiting cameras thinking about what he or she is going to say. Try to capsule it in a sentence. It is easier to do that if you think about how to put a "therefore" at the end of your first sentence and make "therefore" the beginning of your second and last sentence.

What's a "therefore"? Let me explain.

President Johnson loathed having long-winded assistants or visitors regale him with what he already knew. He would affectionately admonish his garrulous aides by telling them a story:

Sam Rayburn, the powerful Speaker of the House in the Eisenhower and Kennedy years, once had a momentary falling out with Franklin D. Roosevelt (when Rayburn was merely a committee chairman). One of Rayburn's colleagues was going to visit FDR and Rayburn urged him to find out what the President thought about the controversy. The congressman obligingly agreed. Later that day, the congressman visited Rayburn's office and said, "Now, when the President had me enter the Oval Office, I told him . . ." and he launched on an interminable recital of what he had said to FDR.

Finally Rayburn exploded: "I don't give a good goddamn about what you told FDR, but I damn sure want to know what Roosevelt told you!"

LBJ would tell this story with relish. Whenever an aide embarked upon a windy report, LBJ would stare him down and say, "Remember Sam Rayburn? Therefore, therefore." What he meant was *get to the point*. Therefore: your conclusion.

Therefore, I counsel my congressional friends, when they know they are about to be asked questions by newsmen, especially those with cameras attached, to have their "therefore" ready. For instance:

"I just finished a twenty-minute meeting with the President." (And now the "therefore.") "I told the President I could not agree that the base in Slippery Rock should be closed because it is too vital to our national defense."

The congressman (or senator) will surely be on the evening news that night if the subject is at all important, because (1) he specified with precision the presence of a controversy, and (2) he said it so briefly no editor can fool with it.

Another way to assure yourself of a fifteen-second spot on the networks is to put your "therefore" in an epigrammatic frame. No editor can resist keeping it inside the story.

A senator believes in more money for the armed forces. Leaving a hearing room in which the defense budget is being debated, he wants to make clear his commitment to that cause. A mike is thrust under his mouth and the camera eye gapes at him.

Question: "Senator, is the defense budget going to be increased?"

Answer: (The "therefore" up front and dressed in spice.) "If I have my way, it will. The world is on fire and all we did today was sit in there playing a broken fiddle."

The senator has made three points: (1) he is for a strong defense; (2) he considers the world situation serious; (3) the committee is unable to make any decisions.

The networks will have interviewed a dozen or so senators from that same hearing. You can wager this senator will make the show. He was brief. He had a "therefore." And he said it with some color.

During a committee hearing in the spring of 1981, a House Education Subcommittee was interrogating the Secretary of Education. At issue were severe budget cuts designed by Budget Director David Stockman and offered in the new financial package submitted by President Reagan.

Congressman Peter Peyser, a Democrat from Westchester County in New York, seemed to understand the necessity of putting into a succinct line his critique of the Reagan budget and its architect, Mr. Stockman.

To Secretary Terrel Bell, Peyser said: "In many ways, Mr. Secretary, I feel very sorry for you. President Reagan doesn't understand what is involved and David Stockman really doesn't care. He is like a bomber pilot flying high: He can't see the bodies he's destroying."

When the evening news show appeared that day, the editors had a ton of film to consider. Congressman Peyser survived the cut. His three brief sentences captured the color of the hearings.

Don't rely on intuition or inspiration to keep you flying. You may feel confident you can wing it, but lights and camera can disrupt even the sternest discipline. You may get flustered, you may ramble, and you will be a winning candidate for the outtake, seen only by the film editor and the guy who sweeps up the cutting-room floor.

Think, think, think. Turn over a sentence or two in your mind. How can you phrase your thought to capture public attention? If you have time, jot it down. Read it over several times. If you have a firm grasp of the essentials of what you want to say, your increased confidence will keep you from disarray when the camera points at you.

Television magnifies everything. If you could be given the choice of only one asset to take before the camera, you would be right to select believability. Even if you don't speak with precision or brevity, if you express your thoughts with complete believability, you are ahead of the game.

A number of corporations are using real people rather than actors in their TV ads: farmers, for example, who extol the virtues of cars or machinery or even household goods. The reason: While the farmer might stumble over his words, or speak them in rural accents, what comes out is real, not faked. And that is the shining virtue the advertising agency is searching for. Whatever is contrived—in a commercial message or a speech or in a comment by a public figure or businessman—can claim little value.

It is one of the ironies of human nature that those very people, public officials, great corporate captains, civic leaders, who ought to be able to communicate through television are often ill-prepared and, what is worse, even when prepared cannot present a lucid, believable, winning speech or comment.

Consider the history of speechmaking over the recent modern era and try to catalogue those leaders who pierced the barriers of public indifference or inattention to make their mark on a nation.

In the English-speaking democracies over the last forty years the three leaders who by some magical linkage connected the people to their dreams were Winston Churchill, Franklin Roosevelt, and—for a brief moment—John Kennedy. The constant in each man was a vision embodied in voice and prose. Could Clement Attlee have summoned from that island kingdom a courage to match the crisis as Churchill did? Could Tom Dewey have steered the United States through dangerous years as Roosevelt did? Would Richard Nixon have inspired the country to an idealism of the sort that John Kennedy epitomized and conveyed?

Franklin Roosevelt was the master of radio communication. He overcame all opposition because he had the ready skill to converse believably with the American people. His unique asset was his voice, Ivy League-accented, the legacy of his patrician upbringing. He spoke oracularly, with rolling vowels and a voice timbre pitched a touch high but amazingly resonant.

My mother, who was apolitical and had difficulty remembering who was mayor of her hometown (Houston), was enrapt by Roosevelt. Whenever he spoke, she was perched by the radio, embraced and mesmerized by every Rooseveltian word. Had FDR asked his audience to slit their wrists, my mother would have uncomplainingly headed for the bathroom to find the nearest razor. Such was his power that in the television age, he could have been elected king.

In the television era, only John Kennedy knew with apparently genetic instinct how to handle the medium. He was young, handsome, slim. He was the first of the cool politicians, with a controlled style. He never grinned; he smiled. He never shouted; he spoke conversationally. His passions were always in harness. He was the great sculptor of the urbane line, the sardonic response. He was in command. Since Kennedy, most of the national public leaders, including subsequent Presidents, have been unable to convey a sense of force, of eloquence, of wit or style, with the exception of Ronald Reagan.

Richard Nixon was always suspect. Beads of perspiration had a way of populating his forehead even though the temperature of the room might have been Arctic. There was a hint of the plastic in his gestures; how often can a man make a Checkers speech and get away with it? Nixon's smile would appear to light for a mini-second on his lips and dart away like a frightened minnow in disagreeable waters.

Nixon's defect on television is one that ought to be studied by any serious student of televised communication. Charles de Gaulle unknowingly pinpointed Nixon's difficulty when he wrote of "the number of pretensions in which the statesman has to indulge . . . the devious methods demanded by the art of government."

Nixon's problem was a lack of believability. Well, one might say, why, if he was unbelievable, did he have such great success at getting elected and reelected? Remember, in 1968 he won by a margin of only one half of one percent of the vote, at a time when Hubert Humphrey had come off the Chicago convention disaster (in late August, just two months before the election) deserted by the liberal wing of the Democratic party, struggling desperately to make up lost ground, coming from thirty points behind in the polls to lose by only a sliver.

In 1972, George McGovern was simply out of the mainstream of American political thought, though he was and is a gentle, good man, warm and compassionate.

Nixon looked uncomfortable on television. Taut as a drumskin, he was incapable of looking relaxed. Whenever he spoke there was an aura of hidden motives, as if he were trying to mask what he really felt. A review of past Nixon television appearances reveals a very private man straining to be something he believed himself not to be; yet he persisted in displaying what he thought people wanted. Watching Nixon on TV, one comes away with the notion that he was onstage, delivering a falsely based characterization in a fabricated manner: the forced smile, the cracking of a stern demeanor and then the quick reassembly of the shattered parts, the ponderous homily, the awkward turns as he grazed the edges of travesty.

It has always been my view that Nixon lost the debate with Kennedy that very first night they confronted each other in 1960. And he lost it when his fierce visage glared from the screen and the camera picked up his youthful opponent, smiling confidently, almost amusedly, at the nervous Nixon.

Gerald Ford, possibly one of the most likeable and companionable men ever to hold the job of Chief Executive, simply could not get an entire paragraph into place. The words he spoke became gargoyles which he approached hesitantly and fearfully, edging around them and occasionally tripping over the syllables. One may muse how this cheerful, decent man ever managed to preside so long over his congressional district and to rise to the leadership of his party in the House without learning and practicing the art of speaking before a camera.

As one who was and is genuinely fond of Gerald Ford and finds him immensely alert and intelligent, readily accessible to those around him, able to offer his views in sensible and persuasive fashion, I was continually surprised to find him on television seemingly incapable of speaking a complete thought without groping and searching. While the ability to utter sentences that parse is not in itself so important an asset, the outward evidence of an untroubled line of thought—emerging through the speaker's voice and apparent conviction—is crucial. The rhythm and balance of Ford's presentation was always marred by the lurchings of his speech. It is difficult to inspire, much less persuade, if the audience wants to reach into the speaker's throat with tongs to grasp the next dozen words and pull them out. I wanted so much for him to do better, because I believed him to be a good President.

Lyndon Johnson, fierce and dominating in private meetings, a formidable figure cutting through opposition as a scythe levels a meadow, became a boring grandfather on television. A boisterous campaigner on the stump, he affected a diffidence on television that served only to induce an eye-glazing weariness in all who listened. LBJ is an example of the public man who substitutes for his own singularity of persuasive force a calm he perceives as "Presidential." Johnson felt he ought to smooth out his rough edges, lower his voice—sometimes almost to a whisper—and he picked his way through words as carefully as city folks navigate a field strewn with cow droppings.

Once or twice he did rise to the moment. His most celebrated and triumphant TV appearance was his famous "We shall overcome" speech to a joint session of Congress. This time, what he felt poured out of his gut and transfixed a nation. But in most of his public speeches he was almost dainty—and that word would be found in no one's description of the immense power that seemed to radiate from his pores.

Somewhere in LBJ was a restless political animal raging to get out of that eyelid-drooping facade picked up by the camera. It baffled explanation that he was never able to convey on screen the magnanimity he carried inside him. In a time when the Vietnam War unfolded night after night in the American home, it became his epic—and politically fatal—flaw.

In his presidential television appearances, Jimmy Carter, a quick study, masterly in his command of the facts, had a sing-song delivery and a curious way of popping his eyelids at the end of a sentence. In a close-up this took on the characteristics of a tic. After a while viewers came to wait for the climax of a thought, and sure enough, the eyes popped. I wondered why Carter never studied the tapes of his TV appearances to correct this very distracting mannerism. He also had a habit of dropping his voice level at the end of a sentence, trailing off rather than emphasizing. These all added up to an on-camera image that elicited a grudging ear to listen and a discontented eye to watch in living rooms all over the country.

Most of us remember Senator Edward Kennedy addressing the Democratic National Convention in 1980. On that evening redolent with the remembrance of his two brothers and the legacy of his own dogged, courageous primary campaign, his speech was flawlessly constructed and delivered. Kennedy used the aid of transparent glass TelePrompTers, two glass rectangles mounted on a slim metal holder, one to his right, one to his left. These prompters are unobtrusive and indeed not even visible to the television audience. Therefore, Kennedy appeared to be speaking without notes. He had mastered the prose, and followed the paragraphs without mishap, mounting to a climax that stirred the audience both in the hall and in their homes all over the land. It was a stunning performance. Yet Ted Kennedy, on the stump and before other convention groups, more often than not fixes his gaze on his written text, seldom raising his head to confront his audience. On April 1, 1981, he addressed the Communications Workers of America. His speech was clearly a carefully drafted document, aimed to persuade his audience. But all one saw on television was a thick forest of brown hair.

The reason, I surmise, is a simple one: Kennedy had not familiarized himself with the text in advance. He had not with rigorous preparation and determined effort committed that speech to his mind and tongue. As a result, when he rose he had no choice but to bury himself in the text. What was a sublime and moving experience at the Democratic National Convention became an exercise in tedium at the CWA assembly. Lack of preparation is an oft-committed sin of omission, and the speaker, as well as the audience, loses by it.

Keep in mind that these are all public men, hardened by the experience of years in the public arena. They could not have risen in the political world without being aware of their mistakes and quickly correcting them. And yet the largest potential weapon in their arsenal, their speaking skills, remained impervious to criticism by aides and counselors. From personal knowledge, I am aware that continued entreaties to LBJ to change his style from the artificial (which he assumed) to the natural (which was his own) went in one presidential ear and out the other. Somehow, somewhere, he fastened on the theory that what had brought him unprecedented success as a parliamentary commander was not suitable in the leader of the free world. So he junked the source of his strength and relied instead on something he was not—an error of judgment he never fully retrieved.

Ronald Reagan, with long years of experience before the camera, has learned the craft of communication as few other leaders before him. His voice is rich, innocent of accent or regional tint. His career as an actor has endowed him with gifts of delivery unmatched by his contemporaries. And he understands the cruelties of television.

If you will recall the debate between President Carter and Ronald Reagan in the late days of 1980, perhaps you would agree that there was, as in the Kennedy-Nixon debates, one crucial moment when the debate began to slide out of the hands of one and into the other's. It was that oh-so-brief moment when, as Carter began to repeat charges against his opponent, Reagan leaned forward, grinned widely, and said, "There you go again." It was such a human response, the sort of laughing accusation a next-door neighbor might make. It blurred Carter's arguments, and surprised him as well. He never really recovered.

In his first national address as President, Reagan spoke about the economy. This is a subject guaranteed to faze the most knowledgeable. Listening to a speech about economics, replete with arithmetic and abstruse jargon, may be the only sure cure for insomnia. LBJ once remarked that making a speech about economics was "like pissing down your trouser leg. It makes you feel warm but your audience doesn't know what the hell you are doing."

Reagan gave a vivid demonstration of how powerful is his gift of speaking on February 5, 1981, when he addressed a nationwide audience.

Here are his first few paragraphs:

> I am speaking to you tonight to give you a report on the state of our nation's economy.
>
> I regret to say that we are in the worst economic mess since the Great Depression. A few days ago I was presented with a report I had asked for—a comprehensive audit, if you like it; I didn't like it, but we have to face the truth and then go to work to turn things around. And make no mistake about it, we can turn them around.

I am not going to subject you to the jumble of charts, figures, and economic jargon of that audit but rather will try to explain where we are, how we got there, and how we can get back.

First, however, let me just give a few "attention getters" from the audit. The federal budget is out of control and we face runaway deficits, of almost $80 billion for this budget year that ends September 30. That deficit is larger than the entire federal budget in 1957, and so is the almost $80 billion we will pay in interest this year on the national debt.

No attempt here to be eloquent, merely clear; no attempt to be an orator, but only to be lucid and understood.

I would surmise that the President wrote much of the prose himself, using words and voice spacings he felt comfortable with. There are no big words, perhaps because Reagan may judge himself more at home with short, everyday words rather than transported on the flights of a speechwriter's fancy.

Note the use of the phrase "economic mess." No delicate pirouette here, but language everyone understands. And then the line that lays out what he intends to say: "I . . will try to explain where we are, how we got there, and how we can get back." Give him a grade of A. It is an eminently sufficient summary.

What his speaking form makes clear is that he is at ease with what he is saying. That conversational comfort comes through to the audience so that they feel consoled—despite the bleak, calamitous projections he is offering—by the congenial manner of the message.

He made effective use of visual aids, two simple charts explaining revenue and expenditures, easy to read and quickly understood. Reagan explained briefly the meaning of the charts and how that was relevant to his message.

No other President since JFK has so dominated the television screen. Ronald Reagan knows one must be interesting to be heard and one must be engaging to be listened to and understood.

Marshall McLuhan's famous maxim is real and true: "The medium is the message." Reagan takes McLuhan one step further. People like to hear him talk, for he is not threatening to their well-being and he comes across like the public's favorite TV character, attractive, easy-voiced, comfortable.

Yet the words on paper give little hint of how they sound as they fall from his lips, measured, cleanly stated, without hesitancy. All those years of acting, and of countless speeches before all kinds of audiences, have sharpened in Ronald Reagan an ability thoroughly suited to the small screen in the American living room.

In short, President Reagan is prepared to speak, has trained himself to speak well, and constantly corrects what is wrong. That, essentially, is what speaking in public is all about, especially before a TV camera.

Television is the bully pulpit that Theodore Roosevelt conceived of in the early years of the century, and its use has never been fully explored by any American President, though John F. Kennedy grasped its significance. President Reagan may well exploit this medium in ways that could have a fundamental impact on how he is judged by history and by his constituents.

Corporate leaders, businessmen, education and labor leaders have the opportunity, through closed-circuit television, to speak to their peers, their employees, and their colleagues. They can achieve a rapport with those whom they wish to persuade beyond the capacity of leaders in earlier years when television was not available.

Television defers to the knowledgeable speaker, to the person who appreciates the gaping difference between a large assembly hall and the intimacy of the 21-inch screen.

* * *

I tried, vainly, to persuade President Johnson to make television his rostrum for explanation, for education, for convincing the public that his decisions were wise and of long-term benefit to the American family.

I proposed a plan for a series of ten-minute telecasts to be aired at 10:00 P.M. Eastern Standard Time. The ten-minute limit was not casually suggested. It is long enough to say what needs to be said, but not so long as to blot out favorite entertainment programs. The networks could have easily delayed the start of their regularly scheduled shows for ten minutes without having to cancel entire programs. Hell has a congenial climate by comparison to the wrath of viewers whose favorite sit-com is preempted by a mere President discoursing on the fate of their lives.

My plan was to have the public informed well in advance that the President would not exceed the threshold of tedium. (Ten minutes extracted from the regular television schedule is tolerable, but presidential television advisors must *never* schedule the President at the same time as a popular sporting event. This is blasphemy.) The audience would know that after ten minutes they could settle back to whatever program they were expecting to enjoy.

I suggested that the President review Vietnam in four separate telecasts. The first: Why we are in Vietnam and why it is important to the security of the nation and the families directly affected by the war. Second, how are we doing? Third, is it possible to reconstruct Vietnam peacefully and are we prepared to do it? And fourth, is there the possibility of lasting peace after the fighting has been concluded, and is that a worthy cause to support?

I suggested that the President make similar broadcasts about other difficult problems the nation faced. For instance, the question of pollution and the damage to our environment: the injury to the national economy and health if pollution were allowed to consume all that was clean and fresh in the land. This needed to be explained in simple, understandable language. Issues of crime, urban sprawl and waste, the evil legacies of inflation, and other hard-to-grasp and even harder-to-solve problems would be suitable for this forum.

The use of television as a rostrum was essential to this kind of leadership—the President as educator-communicator, speaking to the people, explaining, simplifying, pointing out problems, and offering solutions that would involve the public in their long-range implementation.

He could not invade the TV screen too often or he might debase his appearances with repetition. If familiarity indeed breeds contempt, there was a fine line to be drawn between maintaining mystery and fulfilling need. The more a leader visits the living rooms of his constituency, the less exotic is his aura and the less attentive the hospitality.

Moreover, the President must choose his subjects carefully. His crisis speeches—when he has a specific and urgent necessity to communicate with the people about a clear-cut concern demanding immediate action—must be set apart from appearances intended to educate the public.

Impact and receptivity are important elements in the leader's public report card. Those to whom he speaks, those he tries to lead, are also those who grade him.

But the requisite without which all is lost is the ability of the leader to speak reasonably, amiably, and believably, and if possible, though it is mystifyingly elusive, to be inspiring.

I was never able to convince President Johnson of the wisdom of this educational approach.

President Johnson never really felt at home in front of a television camera.

Like many a politician bred to fight and speak in local union halls, party clubhouses, and spacious arenas before large groups of people, LBJ never felt comfortable staring at a red light atop some contraption with a single lens that was staring back at him. It was too drained of human juices, too lacking in the stir and stomp of a public responding to his exhortations.

Moreover, if he wasn't speaking in a hall of some kind or on a platform out in the open, he would rather be nose-to-nose with an ally, enemy, or undecided friend, in the one-on-one persuasion technique that he loved to practice on just about anybody whose vote he needed, whose support he required, or whose affection he sought.

LBJ loved to feel, smell, sense, and touch. He reveled in the personal encounter. He had to hear the audience respond, or to have his quarry up close where he could, like some keen bloodhound nose down on the trail, sniff out a response. There was, to him, something perplexing, something sterile in trying to convince a camera.

There was something else that bothered him.

He was an admirer of John Kennedy's graceful style, particularly on television. Somewhere in the recesses of his mind he had the nagging notion that his television performance would be compared with that of his masterly predecessor, and that thought was enough to unsettle him.

The result was a major loss of opportunity for LBJ. He abandoned the one medium that, when he was in political trouble, might have given him the extra heft he needed to persuade the nation. Because he was uncomfortable with TV, he never attempted to master it.

The intelligent use of television not only by public officials but also by leaders in other arenas has to be carefully studied.

It is no longer suitable, if it ever was, to "read" something on television and expect viewers to be excited or interested or persuaded.

The first step is to make what you say compact. The maxim applies to a President addressing grave matters of state, a business leader exhorting his sales force, a school superintendent rallying her teachers: Leisurely disquisitions lose their momentum.

Those who are on television for whatever reason should understand the large truth of Occam's Razor. This is a relatively obscure rule known mainly to students of philosophy, but its obscurity in no way diminishes its relevance. William of Occam (or Ockham, as it is sometimes spelled) was a Franciscan monk who lived in the fourteenth century. He is not well known today (fourteenth-century sages don't travel well), but he did create what came to be known as Occam's Razor, which in essence said, "Entities are not to be multiplied without necessity." To put it another way: Don't do with more what you can do with fewer.

Every time you make any presentation on television keep Occam's Razor in the forefront of your mind. What can be left out because you have already said it or it is obvious, leave out.

Some of our public officials seem to be learning this lesson. Whatever else may be said about television coverage of the U.S. House of Representatives, I am convinced that the quality of speechmaking in that body is improving in both style and brevity—which only admirers of the turgid and interminable will find regrettable. With the advent of television in the House, even though the members cannot be sure of how many attentive viewers they have, the mere awareness that someone is watching out there is bound to curb the oratorical flourishes.

This is not a question suitable for consideration only by public officials. With cable television spreading throughout the nation, and with access to cable channels expanding rapidly, anyone who feels obliged, for whatever reason, to pass a word along to the community will be able to reach his or her fellow inhabitants with amazing ease.

The second step is to consider the response you want from the viewing audience. If you are trying to win them to your point of view, you must make that viewpoint as attractive as you can. You must build upon a well-reasoned foundation. Cite the problem, sound the alarm where it threatens, and propose a course of action to solve it. You may reproach those who oppose or disagree with you, but you must always consider the feelings of the people you are trying to enlist in your cause.

Third, you must remember that in a large hall a reasonable amount of body movement is perfectly acceptable, sometimes even required. But in the confines of a viewer's living room, the television camera captures you with a more brutal scrutiny than you may like. It is fine to express passion in your cause, but without flailing of arms and head. On television, passionate belief is better expressed by a gaze or an emotional inflection of a phrase than by an outthrust fist or jaw.

Fourth, and hardest to learn: To win and hold audience attention, you must try to make everything you say interesting. Alas, there is no formula readily available: X units of content plus Y units of emotional appeal times Z units of persuasiveness equals Audience Interest. You can learn only from experience before a camera, mistakes made and never repeated, trial and error.

I am always a bit amused when an actor in an interview declares that he never watches himself (or herself) on the screen. I suspect this restraint is born of a press agent's imagination, to let the fans know the actor is a modest person, untainted by ego.

The fact is that anyone who appears on television would be well advised to try to watch a tape of that experience. You learn by what you see yourself doing. Do you fidget? Do your hands clasp and unclasp as you speak? Where you thought you were expressing certainty, did you actually grimace? Do you blink incessantly? Do your eyes wander as you speak? Does your mouth droop? Or do you have a habit of smiling at the end of each sentence even though you have just predicted Armageddon at two o'clock next Tuesday? Does your voice waver? Do you drop your voice when it ought to rise?

On a television talk show have you ever heard the introduction of a guest by the host and seen the camera close in on the one being introduced? Do you sometimes see a wan smile appear, then disappear and appear again as anxiety grows? Sometimes the guest seems to be weighing whether or not to go into an "aw shucks, you're too generous" routine when in truth, you suspect, the inner self is boiling because the laurels are too sparsely distributed.

Take careful note of your behavior when you think the camera is not on you. Recently, an important government official was a guest on a television network press conference. He was apparently ignorant of the significance of the red light on the live camera. When the interviewer was speaking, the official began to scratch himself, unaware that every curl of his wiggling fingers was in full screen view of the audience. It did diminish somewhat his efforts at statesmanship a few seconds later.

Errors noted are usually errors not committed again. We learn by watching what we do, and when we do it, and how we do it.

To sum up: Be prepared. Know what you intend to say. If you are using a TelePrompTer in a studio, go over your remarks as often as possible before the red light on the camera goes on. Speak easily; don't try to force anything. Don't get cute or elocutionary. Don't be ponderous. Be yourself. Unease transmits itself to an audience faster than a viral contagion. Study your defects and correct them. Relax. Place friends next to the camera and talk to them; let the camera be simply an eavesdropper.

Why is it that some believe the mere fact of their appearance on television is sufficient to impress and convince their listeners? At the last conference of the Supreme Soviet, after about five minutes of televising the speech of Chairman Brezhnev, the Russian TV camera switched to a studio where a TV announcer actually read the rest of the Chairman's two-hour speech. Chairman Brezhnev reappeared on Russian screens for the last two minutes of his speech, possibly to certify that he had made it through without collapsing.

This designated-hitter format, right out of George Orwell's novels, may be suitable for the USSR, where they can be sure no one will call or write in to protest. But in democratic societies, no one would listen patiently to a reader plodding through a fat text, ignoring everything except the drone of his own voice.

And yet, how often have you watched officials of the government, leaders in labor, business, education, special-interest groups, testifying on television before congressional committees? And how often do these high-powered witnesses—sitting before the microphone, aware that cameras are on them—bury their heads in a thick sheaf of documents and drone on, as they read with fixed gaze every line of every page without so much as a nod to those who are listening?

Many handsomely paid executives, lawyers, professional people, even elected and nonelected government officials who surely should know better, obviously believe themselves exempt from the rules of persuasion. There is no attempt to engage the interest of those to whom they are speaking, no attempt to leaven the bulky written pages with any form of human contact—even though their audience is a committee they are trying to persuade to their point of view, not to mention countless others watching in front of TV sets. The congressmen and senators who are duty-committed to sit through these dreary recitals are earning their public keep during such hearings. Viewers are not so duty-bound. They can turn to other channels.

There are lessons here for business executives who testify before committees of Congress or state legislatures or any other group they must report to or persuade.

The first lesson is: Don't read your presentation in its entirety. Most businessmen or industrial leaders will prepare a long, often dreary, recital of facts and logic, and—to the regret of those who listen—will read the whole bloody text.

The second lesson is: By editing your oral presentation to more sensible limits, you will gain more time to answer your listeners' questions. In the question period you can expand on your oral comments, and offer more detailed explanations of your edited text.

Edit. Prune. Extract everything you wish to emphasize and reassemble those thoughts in your oral presentation. If you have a fifty-page document you are presenting for the record, you ought to *speak* only some ten pages. This is essential if you wish to be persuasive.

VII

LANGUAGE

How to compose your speech to achieve your objective

Some years ago I attended the Indian Film Festival in New Delhi. It was a most impressive visit for me. As the leader of the United States delegation to the festival, I was obliged to attend several conferences and seminars. At one of the latter, a well-known Asian film expert, fluent in English, rose to speak about the worldwide infatuation with film.

Here is a paragraph from his speech:

> The theory that there exists a Cartesian polarity between arbitrary aesthetic signs and total realism necessarily led to quantitative conclusions and meaningless oppositions: the proliferation of detail as against metaphysical truth, where quality cannot be seized, the fluidity of *mise-en-scène* as against metre of montage, the existential tension of suspense in Hitchcock, as against the tragic release from pity and fear.

127

I cite this as an example of an attempt to impress an audience with a combination of words that should never have been spoken, or written, or even imagined.

What one says is as important as how one says it. However, while it is possible that a badly drafted speech may receive renewed life in the throat of an inspired orator, it is also true that a poor speaker can infect a brilliantly composed speech with the rickets.

It was reported that in the last few days of his life Benjamin Disraeli, ill and haggard, sat up in his bed to correct the proofs of his final speech. "I will not go down to posterity speaking bad grammar," he said.

All of this is preface to emphasizing the importance of preparing a speech so that it reads well, has glimpses of style, is clear in its message, and offers ample opportunity for the speaker to inform, persuade, convince, and/or entertain.

The first step in preparing a written speech, whether you intend to read it verbatim, speak it from notes, or memorize it, is to know what you want to accomplish and then to plan carefully how you will achieve your goal.

There are three parts to a speech, though they do not necessarily follow in precise order, and they may be repeated within the speech.

The first is some humor or wit, some attempt to lighten the more serious aspects of your message—if it is appropriate to do so. If it is not, leave the humor out.

The second is to present convincingly the purpose of your speech.

The third is to frame your speech in prose that conveys the

substance you want your audience to grasp, and to do it as interestingly as you possibly can.

One helpful suggestion for drafting a speech is to recall the tenets of a great teacher of acting, Charles Jehllinger, who taught for many years at the American Academy of Dramatic Arts in New York. His pupils included Spencer Tracy, Robert Walker, Rosalind Russell, Katharine Hepburn, and Kirk Douglas.

He admonished his students to be ever conscious, as they recited their lines, of *thought, theme,* and *mood.* I refer to it as TTM.

Consider this acronym as you prepare what you want to say.

What is the *Thought* you want to convey?

What is the *Theme* of your presentation?

What *Mood* do you want to evoke?

TTM can be a guide for you, as valuable to the most inexperienced speaker as it is to an aspiring actor. While you may not have considered the similarity, it does exist: As an actor is performing on a stage to engage an audience, so are you when you rise to speak.

While it is true that the actor is speaking lines written by someone else, and you are probably saying what you have composed yourself, there is a more than casual connection between the objectives of the actor and your own.

You don't have to be an actor in the professional sense of the term, but you are performing—that is, like the actor, your object is to be believed by those who listen to you, to awake their interest, to gain a rapport with the audience. You don't have to win an Oscar or a Tony with your efforts. But you do have to be aware that you are involved in a performance.

Long ago I was enchanted by and became a disciple of

Descartes. His rules of logic, while applying directly to the solving of almost any problem, financial, political, entrepreneurial, or scientific, can also inform your preparation of a speech. They make a corollary to TTM.

The rules are:

1. Discard everything except that which you know to be true.
2. Break the subject down into as many parts as possible.
3. Start with the easier parts and progress to the hardest to understand.
4. Summarize.

Think for a minute how Descartes can aid you in preparing a speech.

Use that which you know to be true and can certify as such.

Consider what you want to say to the audience and divide it into simple parts. Keep in mind the need to make your audience understand what you are saying. When President Reagan made his economic speech to the nation, he started with simple equations and visual aids which provided a foundation for an examination of the terribly complex issue of inflation.

If you are able to write a speech worth making, by summarizing briefly you can give your thoughts additional impact. You may begin your speech with a summary of what you intend to say, and end your speech with a summary of what you have said. But a summary should be little more than a sentence or two.

If I were asked to draft a presidential speech on an economic program to be presented to the people, this is how (using the advice of Descartes) I would begin:

Tonight, my fellow citizens, I present to the American people a plan designed to lift the quality of our economy, so the future of the American family will be safer, healthier, more meaningful and more prosperous.

This plan which I will present to the Congress will achieve five goals:

1. It will increase the productivity of American industry.

2. It will provide incentive for factories, business, and corporations to increase jobs, with specific emphasis on teenage employment as well as on shrinking the rate of adult unemployment.

3. It will halt the spiral of inflation and bring that contagion down to gentler levels.

4. It will generate more vigorous American trade abroad.

5. It will encourage American business to renovate old equipment, and design and order new equipment.

Higher productivity, more jobs, increased export trade, modernizing American industry, reducing inflation: That is our program. That is what we are resolved to do. And here is our plan for doing it, a plan that requires the cooperation of each of you listening to me tonight.

Note that the speech immediately breaks down what is to follow under five different headings. It summarizes the task.

The speech would then detail each part of the plan: why it is being offered, how it will be implemented, what the results will be, and how the individual American family will benefit.

After the details are itemized, the speech should once more repeat the goals of the plan and summarize what will be done.

As an example of a conclusion:

This nation, like much of the world, is engaged in a struggle with obscure and hard-to-understand issues. All of these mysterious and complex problems crowd in on us, divide us and frustrate us. Some of us may think the future is too bleak, with no redeeming hope.

But a free society must never allow itself to be baffled by confusion. We in the United States are not afraid of tomorrow. Political freedom, to sustain itself, requires risk and innovation. If we understand what ails us, stand together in common cause and common purpose, we can find our way out of this momentary dark moment in our history.

What I am offering you tonight is a blueprint for your family's economic well-being. It will command us to stick together. It will involve, in a cooperative way, your family, your neighbors, and your representatives in Congress. With traditional and unbreakable American resolve, we will achieve what we need and must have.

We will increase productivity in American industry.

We will provide incentives so that factories and plants can increase jobs, for young teenagers and adults as well.

We will halt the spiral of inflation.

We will generate more American trade abroad.

We will modernize American industry.

We will do all this because we will do it together.

With Descartes's guidance, we have shaped a speech that tries to be clear and comprehensible, that attempts to lay out complex problems in doses easy to assimilate, and that summarizes frequently the goals of the plan so that even those who listen with half an ear will grasp the essence of both the plan and the plea.

This is an example of how it is possible to deal with abstruse and speculative matters in language that is both accessible and revealing.

The composition of a speech begins with the objective of the speech. What is your goal? What do you want your audience to feel and think when you have finished?

The essential first step, then, is the careful marking of the objective.

The more advance time you spend in defining what you want to achieve, the greater the possibility you will achieve it. Therefore, clear the way for your speech with as precise a design as you can construct.

At the 1980 Democratic National Convention in New York, Senator Edmund Muskie of Maine, himself a former contender for his party's presidential nomination, approached the rostrum to introduce a film depicting the life of the late Hubert Humphrey. I was one of those counseling Senator Muskie on the organization of his remarks.

The senator determined that he wanted to lift the spirits of those present with a brief speech about the personal vibrancy of the former Vice President. Appropriately, Muskie aimed at raising the emotional level of the assembly. He wanted the spirit of Humphrey to invade the hall, arousing the delegates as if Humphrey had returned to life with all his talent for the stirring of passionate beliefs in fervent causes.

Ed Muskie, when he is moved, is one of the finest platform speakers in the land, with a resonant deep voice, illustrative and reasonable. He understands the lilt of movement as few speakers do.

This is an abridged version of what he said that evening, an example of a speech delivered with its purpose realized. As you read it, watch for the deliberate rhythms of its prose. Long sentences are followed by short ones. Explanatory sentences are succeeded by hammer-strong briefer ones. In the very first paragraph there is a natural progression from Humphrey's sterling qualities to the introduction of his name.

Ask yourself how you would improve on the balancing of the cadence, and on the recounting of what Humphrey stood for and what he believed in and why he was Humphrey.

Each line in this speech was carefully constructed. This is not to say it was ideally constructed or could not be improved. But it was not put together casually. Any speech that aspires to be a good speech should be attended to with care, given thought and time and not hobbled by uneven concentration or inattention to detail.

My Fellow Citizens:

I come before you tonight to speak of love and laughter, of wisdom and warmth, of duty and honor. I come before you to measure a terrible loss and to remind you of a joyous legacy. I come to speak of Hubert Humphrey.

He came out of Dolan, South Dakota, the son of a druggist, with no hint of what lay in store for him. He came to political life brimming over with ideals that may seem a bit old-fashioned today, though in fact courage and humor are never out of style.

Almost thirty-two years ago to this very hour, in another Democratic convention in Philadelphia, this thirty-seven-year-old mayor of Minneapolis, and a candidate for the United States Senate, rose to his feet and with a single speech electrified the entire nation. The sound of his voice became the herald and the inspiration of both a party and a country. He spoke the words that lit up a dark corner of the American soul.

Hear the voice of Hubert Humphrey in 1948: "There are those who say to you, 'We are rushing this issue of civil rights.' I say we are 172 years late. There are those who say, 'This issue of civil rights is an infringement of states' rights.' The time has arrived for the Democratic party to get out of the shadow of states' rights and walk forthrightly into the bright sunshine of human rights. People—human beings—this is the issue of the twentieth century."

From that moment on, Hubert Humphrey became a force for decency in the American political arena. Until the very last hour of his life on this earth, the decency in Humphrey never wavered or failed.

This hall tonight is crowded with those who knew Hubert so very well. Can we not see and hear him now, vibrating with ideas, spilling over with the enthusiasm that would have broken the shield of the grumpiest among us?

Behind the infectious Humphrey grin existed a man always in full command of the resources of the most fertile political mind any one of us has ever encountered. No combination of peril and embarrassment would perplex him. No danger could daunt him.

He was an intellectual who spoke the language of the village square. He endured defeat because he believed that defeat was never final and setbacks only momentary. He kept his eye on the distant objective and not the one nearest him.

He was that most peculiar of all public men. He never hated. He never swore vengeance. He embraced his enemies and loved his friends. Where others saw cunning and deceit, he saw possibilities of redemption. Where others grew wary and cautious, he plunged in to do what needed to be done.

Sometimes he was the bearer of unrecognized truth. But eventually, what he declared to be right soon claimed the allegiance of those who saw only dimly what he saw so clearly.

Hubert found barriers not as ugly walls but as lovely hurdles, to be challenged, to be surmounted. And he did it all with grace and skill and wit.

It is shameful that he never became President.

It is an act of national omission that time will never expunge.

What would he have brought to the presidency?

He would have cared, deeply, persistently, lovingly. He would have cared about the sick and the hopeless. He would have felt the deep personal agony that comes to the leader who is able to get inside the gut and heart of those citizens who look to the President as the one and only person whose purpose is guided by their reach for hope.

I can tell you that not a day goes by but what I don't listen and hear that sparkling voice or feel his arm around my shoulder. I was proud, oh God, how I was proud to be his running mate.

What you are now about to see is a short film about Hubert. It will light up your memory, though I daresay your memory of Hubert has never diminished. As you watch, consider this: You will be seeing one of the most fascinating public servants in all the history of this Republic. His like will not be found again in our lifetime. But he did live. He was among us. He gave more than he received. His most durable monument is the love that is banked in our hearts. No man can leave a larger legacy.

There are two methods available to you in the actual creation of a speech. Which one you use depends on how you best can shape what you want to say into a finished speech.

The first method:

Sketch out on paper fairly detailed notes on what you want to convey, the points you want to emphasize and the impression you want to make on your audience. This is essential. Unless you have a clear idea of what you want to say, it is doubtful you will say anything worth remembering.

Then dictate your speech into a tape recorder or to a secretary. By this method, you are speaking to an audience much as you talk conversationally.

Sir Winston Churchill usually prepared his speeches and books by this method. He adapted his singular abilities to the service of the spoken word, and through his rare chemistry of wit and literacy and his classic style of prose construction, many a sentence emerged like a pearl from an oyster shell, finely polished, shining, and symmetrical. Writing many years later about how his poor schoolwork at Harrow had resulted in enforced repetition of classes, including grammar and composition, he said, "I got into my bones the noble structure of the simple English sentence."

The youthful Churchill was, as many of us are, a slow and awkward learner. In his early parliamentary career he was very good at assembling a set speech, carefully prepared in the classic tradition, but he was then something less than an eloquent speaker. Lord Balfour (nephew of a Prime Minister and later the crown's first minister himself) once said of Churchill's early speaking style: "He carried heavy but not very mobile guns."

He also had great skill in editing his own material. He required his publishers to set type for every book, and then would rewrite extensively.

But there are few Churchills in a generation. We lesser mortals must be content with a literacy less comprehensive and an eloquence less spellbinding.

In your first dictated draft, don't bother to give what you are saying a finished tone. Keep talking. When you are done, have that draft typed. Now, go over it carefully. Extract the repetition that will surely be there. Smooth the rough edges so that the sentences parse, and no explanation is extraneous to your theme. Check over any statistics you use to ensure their accuracy.

With your first draft in hand, speak again into the tape recorder. If there is anything in the speech that gives you problems, revise as you go; that is, stop the tape recorder and make any changes you find necessary. Go through the entire speech adding whatever persuasive elements are required to gain and hold the attention of your audience.

You will now be ready to decide whether to give your speech from your finished text or to use notes. Go with whichever form makes you feel more comfortable. Keep in mind that as a rule a speech is more effective when delivered from notes than when read from a prepared text. But if you are tense with anxiety and the feeling that you are walking a tightrope without a safety net, you will probably detract less from the quality of your presentation if you opt for the prepared text.

On June 20, 1940, The House of Commons went into secret session to hear the new British Prime Minister. Under the rules of the Commons, no recording of such speeches is ever made. There is no accurate historical accounting of what is spoken by the members. A pity—but then, the Commons has existed for over seven hundred years, sufficient to attest to the durability of the English system without the need for sage counsel from outsiders like me.

Winston Churchill, in all his other appearances in secret sessions during the war, carefully prepared his speeches, wrote them out, and preserved them for his own personal record. But on this June 20, he did not.

What he did do was think about his remarks with the systematic precision he employed, with inveterate success, over the years of his stewardship, and put to paper a series of notes from which he drew his final speech.

Here are the notes (which I have edited for brevity's sake) that Churchill used in that secret-session speech. In the British Archives one may see, written in Churchill's own hand, the scratchy annotations with which he embellished his speech shortly before he rose to deliver it.

Secret Session. House of Commons.

My reliance on it as an instrument for waging war.
More active and direct part for its Members L.D.V.
All this in accordance with past history.
This S.S. a model of discretion.
My view always Govt. strengthened by S.S.
Agree with idea S.S. shd be quite a normal part of our procedure, not associated with any crisis.
Relief to be able to talk without enemy reading.
Quite ready to have other S.Ss., especially on precise subjects.
But I hope not press Ministers engaged in conduct of war too hard.
Mood of the House. Cool and robust.
Speeches most informative. Difficult to betray any secrets disclosed today.
Moore-Brab (Wallesey) Praise.
He was sorry I mentioned expert advisers favored fighting on.
Politicians and Generals,
In last war and this.
Not put too much on the politicians: even they may err.
Goering. How do you class him? He was an airman turned politician.
I like him better as an airman. Not very much anyway.
This supreme battle depends upon the courage of the ordinary man and woman.
Fate of Northern Armies sealed when the G. armoured Divisions curled round their whole communication. Abbeville, Boulogne, Calais.
Not 2 days' food. Only ammunition one battle.
Question of forming Torres-Vedras line.
Quite impossible with Air attack on ports. One in three supply ships sunk.
Situation looked terrible, especially when Belgium gave in.

Give all credit to all three Forces.

Army fought its way back; Navy showed its wonderful reserve power; Air Force rendered naval work possible.

B.E.F. a fine Army. Only 10 Divisions.

Some remarks about Home Defence.

Belisha spoke of 'man the defences and resist the enemy.'

That will play its part; but essence of defence of Britain is to attack the landed enemy at once, leap at his throat and keep the grip until the life is out of him.

We have a powerful Army growing in strength and equipment every day.

Many very fine Divisions.

Vigilant coast watch. Strong defence of ports and inlets.

Mobile Brigades acting on interior lines. Good prospects of winning a victory.

If Hitler fails to invade or destroy Britain he has lost the war.

If enemy coastline extends from Arctic to Mediterranean and we retain sea power and a growing air power it is evident that Hitler, master of a starving, agonized and surging Europe, will have his dangers as well as we.

Attitude of United States. Nothing will stir them like fighting in England.

No good suggesting we are down and out.

The heroic struggle of Britain best chance of bringing them in.

Anyhow they have promised fullest aid in materials, munitions.

A tribute to Roosevelt.

All depends upon our resolute bearing and holding out until Election issues are settled there.

If we can do so, I cannot doubt a whole English-speaking world will be in line together and with the Oceans and with the Air and all the Continents except Europe (RUSSIA).

I do not see why we should not find our way through this time, as we did last.

Question of Ireland. Greatly influenced by a great Army developing here.

Germans would fight in Ireland under great disadvantages.

Much rather they break Irish neutrality than we.

Lastly, say a word about ourselves.

How the new Govt. was formed.

Tell the story Chamberlain's actions.

Imperative there should be loyalty, union among men who have joined hands.

Otherwise no means of standing the shocks and strains which are coming.

I have a right to defend loyalty to the administration and feel we have only one enemy to face, the foul foe who threatens our freedom and our life, and bars the upward march of man.

Note that Churchill made certain his speech would have the coloration of his particular style, a legacy of his close reading of Edward Gibbon and Lord Macaulay in his youth. See the evidence: "Fate of Northern Armies *sealed* when the G. armoured Divisions *curled* round their whole communication." (Italics mine.)

See again the use of a quotable phrase written in the notes: "leap at his throat, and keep the grip until the life is out of him."

And again: "it is evident that Hitler master of a starving, agonized and surging Europe."

These notations verify that Churchill never abandoned his insightful use of the baroque clause, the identifying imprint of

Churchillian prose which vexes his literary critics.

One more important element: His final paragraph was written out in full, so that he would not have to forage for the right words to conclude his presentation to the Commons.

These notes provided Churchill with the framework for his message. He had years of practice, and confidence in his ability to clothe the brief phrases of his notes in oratorical velvet, weaving each note with the one before and the one after in a seamless whole.

Obviously, none of us will be able to duplicate this unique and memorable talent. But what can be learned is the technique of preparation. How successful are the results depends on the time and energy one is ready to invest. It is fair to state that any speech is improved by the diligence of the writer's preparatory work.

The speech you make need not grapple with the profound issues of life and death, the survival of a nation and a civilization, as Churchill's did. But when you report on a corporate plan to your fellow employees or propose a project to your civic organization, the labor required remains the same. It is simply a matter of giving enough thought to what you are going to say, deciding how you will develop your message, and then dictating into a tape recorder.

Finally, when the finished text is done, it is well to recite it once more into the tape recorder, this time for intonation, for inflection, for emphasis given to matters of importance, and for timing.

Listen to the tape over and over again. Make notes on your text where you believe an upbeat tone is required, or where you think you should lower your voice to draw greater attention, by contrast, to what may follow.

The second method:
In this method, you write out in advance what you will

speak. In long hand or on a typewriter, you build your speech as you would a letter, an essay, or a memorandum to a friend whose support is necessary to your cause.

I find this method personally more satisfying because I like to see the words form in front of me. Their appearance is congenial to my purpose, and I am attracted to the serried march of the words as I compose my text. The speech becomes more a companion because I have watched it grow before my eyes.

Some years ago I was selected to present to John D. Rockefeller III the prestigious Jefferson Award of the American Institute of Public Service.

I deliberated for a good many hours over the theme of that presentation. My aim was to encapsule, in less than five minutes, the life of Mr. Rockefeller, and to do so in a fashion calculated to enlighten the audience not only about his work, which all were familiar with, but more notably about the form and force of his character.

My audience would be largely Washingtonian, men and women experienced in politics, literate and informed about current affairs. They would be people who either knew Rockefeller personally or at least were knowledgeable about his life work. Therefore I wanted to give some emotional weight to what I said, above and beyond relating the specifics of his personal performance.

I determined that my theme would be the genetic code of the Rockefeller family, and that family's persistent acceptance of their obligation to a country that had provided them with the means to enormous wealth.

I began to write, bending every word to the purpose of my theme. I found the first draft unsatisfying. It was too long and it lacked continuity.

So I wrote out a second draft and a third. Then I revised the third draft, excising some lines that did not fit and modifying those that needed some small lift.

Finally, I finished the last draft and turned on my tape recorder. I read the speech and then listened carefully to what I had said. I found some phrases awkward on the tongue, such as "commitments flimsily kept." The word *flimsy*, though ideally descriptive for my purpose, works better in print than by voice. I simply could not say "flimsily kept" without slurring. I blotted it out and inserted "not redeemed.' It served my meaning, if not the symmetry, just as well—and I could say it without faltering.

I also had a phrase, "weep real tears," which frankly I liked, but my tongue skidded across the *p* of "weep" and collided with the *r* of "real." I struck out "real tears" and went with "weep" alone. This was not as good a piece of imagery as I had intended, but I felt calmer about saying "weep" than running the risk of skittering across the entire phrase.

I had timed the presentation at three minutes, fifteen seconds. Allowing for any digression I might make at the last minute or any extemporizing I would do, I felt I could handle this presentation within my absolute limit of three minutes forty-five seconds.

This is what I said:

My old boss President Johnson was apt to use the language of Texas ranch-country genetics when he wanted to describe the achievements of a great family. He used to say warmly about the Rockefeller family: [a slight pause] "By god, there is <u>something</u> in the stud."

The Rockefeller family has devoted itself to lifting the <u>excellence</u> and the <u>quality of life</u> in this nation, and around the world. There is a fragile nobility to <u>that</u> kind of goal. It can be so easily shattered by commitments <u>not</u> redeemed [slight pause] or pledges <u>casually</u> neglected. JDR III and his family have achieved their objectives in the unaltered conduct of their lives. Theirs has been a straight clean line through three generations [pause slightly] and is alive and moving in a fourth.

We live in what Shakespeare might have called "a scrambling and unquiet time." It is comforting to a good many people that even so, there are some qualities which are proof against the erosion of excellence.

The worth of JDR III can be measured only if you believe in ancient values, [pause] in the meaning of justice and compassion, [pause] if you can weep at the misery of those who are pressed against the wall because of the meanness of chance over which so few of us have any real control.

No Republic can long survive unless there exists in the community a replenishing supply each generation of honorable men and women who worry not at all about social fads or political fashions. They live by sterner codes. They are unrelieved by moral shortcuts. Mr. Rockefeller and his family belong to this band of caring citizens.

Mr. Rockefeller has won this award not only because of his long and rewarded efforts in population control, but because he has been involved in educating the nation in a number of unpopular issues. As Chairman of the Rockefeller Foundation, he has been a quiet and unobtrusive man. But every day of his life he has been involved in helping others live a better life.

Elbridge Gerry, one of the founding fathers, probably valued the Rockefeller family goal accurately when he said in the birth year of the Republic: "The whole business of life [slight pause] is to serve your country."

It is the best one-line description of Mr. Rockefeller that I know.

Woodrow Wilson had a gift for the phrase that lingers in the mind. Often his speeches were lit with special, memorable passages, such as "the fundamental rights of humanity," or "watchful waiting," as well as "peace without victory." These pithy two- and three-word phrases that people can store up in memory are the essence of vivid, indelible speechmaking.

President Wilson was always conscious of the power of the human voice to plead, amuse, inspire, terrify, soothe, and eventually persuade. He used the spoken word as often as he could, not wishing to rely on the printed message alone. It was he who revived a tradition begun by George Washington and John Adams, and later set aside by Thomas Jefferson (who, though a gifted writer, was not eloquent or even modestly inspiring in speech), to present to the Congress in person the presidential State of the Union message.

To catch the minds of your listeners and force them to remember what you have said is the second highest goal to which a speaker can aspire. The first is to persuade them.

Former Minnesota Senator Eugene McCarthy once said of Hubert Humphrey: "Humphrey's detractors accuse him of talking too much. That is unfair. His fault is that when he says things, he says them in a way that people remember. It's dangerous for a national candidate to say things people remember."

In Franklin Roosevelt's speech on Washington's Birthday in 1942, the old master was in high form as he catalogued grim facts about the war in the jaunty, stylish manner he made so famous. As you read, you can almost hear the patrician accents of his voice:

> From Berlin, Rome and Tokyo we have been described as a nation of weaklings—playboys—who would hire British soldiers or Russian soldiers or Chinese soldiers to do our fighting for us.
> Let them repeat that now!

Let them tell that to General MacArthur and his men.
Let them tell that to the sailors who today are hitting
hard in the waters of the Pacific.
Let them tell that to the boys in the Flying Fortresses.
Let them tell that to the Marines.

This was a typical FDR speech, delivered with high good
humor—and a mailed fist.

It is true that quotable, freshly minted phrases have a way
of winning audiences, but if you are a beginner, or still wres-
tling with the quirks of speaking before groups, keep what you
say as simple as you can.

As you go about composing what you choose to say, keep
some simple pointers in mind:

First, draw up an outline, however brief, of what you want
to get across, including some of the specific points you want
to make.

Second, try not to introduce too many elements into your
speech. That is, don't spread your gospel too thin, with too
many points to make and remember. If you are delivering a
report to your civic group on a number of projects, that is quite
all right. But if you are giving the audience something more
than a list of plans and their implementations, try to eliminate
all but one or two key points.

Third, don't hesitate to seek out people you respect for ideas,
or even phrases you might use. Don't let pride or any other
awkward vice keep you from asking others for their judgment.

Fourth, as you construct your speech, never forget that this is not an exercise in personal indulgence; you are striving to make contact with your audience. Don't hesitate to throw out anything that is excess baggage. (I confess this is my largest sin in speaking, for I find the counsel I give you now the most difficult to follow myself.)

Metaphors, as I can painfully recall, are apt to do a speaker in unless they are carefully crafted. William Safire, the *New York Times* columnist, recounted a story about Senator Everett Dirksen, Republican leader during the LBJ presidency, and his brave attempts to use the metaphor with precision. Safire reported that Senator Dirksen rose in the Senate to say "At last we have a firm hand on the rudder of the ship of state." Granted that this phrase does not break new ground in the field of persuasion, Safire explained: "Dirksen enlisted the power of a nautical metaphor even though his speechwriter was chagrined later to learn that the man with the hand on the rudder would be drowning and nobody would be minding the tiller."

Fifth, hark back to the brief passage from FDR's Washington's Birthday speech. Note the short, shot-slinging sentences. They are spare, without elaborate ornamentation. They are like the hammer that pounds the nail that seals the cask. They are drivingly effective in this short passage, but an entire speech made up of such sentences would be barren. If you compose a long sentence, try to follow it with a shorter one. There is a reason for this recommendation besides rhythmic balance. Unless you are trained in breathing, if you string out too many long sentences you are apt to find yourself gulping in air to refuel your lungs. It is a touch clumsy to do that.

Sixth, use words that are readily understandable, as clear in meaning as you can make them. Seek out every now and then a saucier word than the usual one, to give what you say a brighter tinge. But don't move too quickly in this area; give yourself some practice time, testing gradually your ability to add the spice of a new expression to something that is plainly true.

Seventh, always try to summarize what you have said. Implant in your audience a closing reminder of what you would impress upon their memories.

A MODEST EPILOGUE

What you have just finished reading is not the end-all of learning to speak. But it is a beginning.

If you have now resolved that you want to speak with more authority, with more believability, and with more confidence, go back over this book and make notes about its key points.

The first, essential word to remember is *think*. Think about what you want to say. Think about the audience you will address. Use TTM—Thought, Theme, and Mood—as your guide. Recall Descartes and his rules of discourse.

Think about brevity and the need to be concise.

Think about how you will phrase what you want to say.

Think about how you are going to be as professional as possible. Don't expect to be the "great orator." Be satisfied with knowing you have done better than you thought you could, but always be your most caustic critic. Learn to do better by gauging what you did last.

Practice, practice, practice. Never rise to your feet without having given thought to what you are going to say.

When you use a prepared text, never, never, never speak those words without first making them your friends through constant and persistent attention.

Remember that an audience is composed of human beings subject to the same emotions you feel. Always treat them with the most loving care. Never permit yourself to think of them as mere breathing backboards for your words. Reach out to them; strive to let them know that you care about their feelings.

Speaking well is thinking clearly.

Speaking exceptionally well is thinking with exceptional clarity.

Finally, never allow yourself to believe, even for an instant, that you can succeed without thorough preparation. Not even the classiest professional is able to get away with that.

I can promise you only this: If you take to heart—and mind —what this small volume attempts to convey, the seeds of good speaking are planted.

You are beginning to be ready to Speak Up with Confidence.